Italian text by
Sandro Chierichetti

siena
guide for tourists

Translations by
Studio Sandonà/Milan

EDITIONS R.I.S. BY ITALO ROMBONI/SIENA

Historical artistic note

The fame of Sienna — one of the cities most rightly admired and visited in Italy — is above all tied to the excellent conservation of her historic-artistic center, both of her greatest monuments and those of minor estetic significance but of equal documentary interest. The city, placed upon three hills, is a continuous up and down of narrow and sinuous alleys which lend it an unconfoundable air. Its hilly aspect consents, in many places, a picturesque prospective and fascinating panoramic visions. But let us come right away to the essential lines of her history and art, even if only synthetically.

We know nothing of the origins of Sienna which has in the past been retained Etruscan, Gallic, Roman. Todays critical doubts are a follow-up of a long period in which the Siennese wished to feel themselves sons of Rome. The symbol of the city, a female wolf suckling Romulus and Remus, attest to this along with her coat of arms — the so-called "Balzana" — with its colors of black and white, the colors of the two legendary horses ridden by Aschelus and Senio, sons of Remus, in order to reach this land from Rome and found Sienna. We know for certain that Sienna was Roman during the republican period and that Augustus, in order to preside over and populate her, produced a colony. The name of that village was Sena Julia.

During the beginning of the medieval period, after the Longobard and French domination, a feudal order was imposed with domination by the counts and then by bishops who, during the XIth cent. became true rulers and tutors of the city. Out of the feudal crisis arose, also at Sienna, the Communal civilization, initially favored, later oposed by the bishops. But, once having overthrown the bishop Rainero (1147), the free Siennese community was completely consolidated. From that moment on, until 1555, Sienna constituted one of the two republics in Tuscany (the other being Lucca) who conserved the longest her own autonomy before the political supremacy of Florence.

The government of the Siennese republic was generally made up of oligarchies which changed with the changing of the social equilibrium, dominated, at different times, by the richest and noblest ranks or by the so-called small populace, mostly composed of artisans and merchants. The internal life of Sienna was notably unstable, continually agitated by contestations of families versus factions, so much to that the great religious figures of the city, such as St. Catherine, St. Bernardino, Pope Pio II never tired of pleading the cause of civil peace. Among the many Siennese governments to be remembered in particular are; that of the Nine (1291-1355) which guaranteed the republic a certain internal stability and years of prosperity and cultural exhuberance (see public palace). Almost at the end of the republic, from 1478 to 1512, a rich citizen, Pandolfo Petrucchi, imposed dominion and gave proof of ability and moderation.

As for Sienna's external politics, they were countermarked first by the wars with her feudal neighbors, then with the Umbrian and Tuscan cities and, as already mentioned, above all with Florence, wars which led Sienna to extend her possession in Southern Tuscany and Maremma. The long struggle between the Siennese ghibellines and the Florentine guelf knew alternating phases such, for example, as the Siennese victory at Montaperti (1260), conquered thanks to the heroism of Provenzan Salvani and of Farinata degli Umberti, and the Florentine victory at Colle di Val d'Elsa (1269) where Provenzan Salvani fell. But the war ended with the definitive success of Florence, obtained by the intervention of the Spanish army. The surrender to Spain was preceded by a siege lasting over a year sustained by the brotherhood of the populace before a common enemy, tried by famine, plague and incredible suffering: the 17th April, 1555, Sienna fell after having lost almost two-thirds of her population. Around 700 families, guided by the political refugee Florentine Piero Strozzi, animator along with the Frenchman Biago di Montluc of the Siennese Resistence, exiled themselves at Montalcino where the symbols of the antique republic lasted four more years until July 1559 when, due to the peace of Chateau-Cambrésis, the territory of the Siennese state was included as fief of the crown of Spain in the dukedom, and then grandukedom of Tuscany, then governed by Cosimo I de' Medici. Several ports of the Maremma and Argentario (the so-called State of the Directors) were passed, instead, to the dominion of the spanish viceroy of Naples.

The times of the Siennese Liberal Republic were, also from an artistic point of view, the most florid. In the second half of the 1200's and particularly in the first half of the 1300's those temples and palaces which, still today are the glory of the city, were built: they offer testimony to the local interpretation of that gothic style which was affirming itself everywhere. This very architectonic rigor is also the reflection of the economic prosperity of those times: in fact at Sienna, even before Florence, a mercantile activity of European range was being exercised (favored by the passage, near Sienna, of the "francigena way", that is, the road which reached Gaul from Rome) which consented banking operations of very high profits. For a certain period of time the Siennese bankers collected, in fact, the tithes of pontiffs, and financed princes and kings. In those times our city was filled with house-towers, surrounded by powerful walls (the present circumference is almost 7 kilometers long, including bastions and the fort erected by Cosimo I) having as entrances 8 artistic portals and beautified by public fountains among which, the famous Branda Fountain. The *building enrichment continued into the 1400's and 1500's, long conserving its gothic physionomy with the co-operation of Florentine artists such as Bernardo Rossellino and Giuliano da Maiano, and Siennese such as Antonio Federighi, Francesco di Giorgio Martini and Baldassare Peruzzi: all artists who were together architects, sculptors and sometimes (as with Martini and Peruzzi) painters too; one notes along this line, that Sienna, in every century has boasted masters versed in each of the plastic-figurative expressions.*

As for sculpture, her introduction in the second half of the 1200's coincides with the activity in Sienna of Nicola Pisani and his son Giovanni, whose great artistic skill — where romanesque and gothic are variously intertwined and equilibrated — was followed up by a band of disciples. In the first half of the 1300's Tino di Camaino emerges from the sculptors, creator of a personal style, together hierarartic and refined; later a first-rate star emerges, Iacopo della Quercia, nervous and powerful in his ways, modeller of images rich with moral energy. Many drew inspiration from him, often even valid local sculptors until — and we are now well within the 1400's — two very celebrated Florentine masters donated precious masterpieces to Sienna: we are referring to Ghiberti and Donatello, the latter to whom many Siennese sculptors looked, eminent among them all being Lorenzo di Pietro called "Vecchietta" (old woman). But the true glory of Sienna was her painting field which touched its zenith in the first half of the 1300's. As with her sculpture, we limit ourselves here to remembering only the most prodigious names. During the 1200's the Byzantine tradition prevailed to which is tied the first of the four great Siennese painters, Duccio di Buoninsegna, born shortly after the second half of the century and who created new figurative horizons germinated from his rich, polyhedric spirituality and no less great and prodigious illustrative talent. The second, and perhaps greatest of Sienna's painters is Simone Martini who lived from the late 1200's till 1344, the most unconfoundable visive poet of European gothic art: protagonist of his painting is the line, *creating in chromatic space that which melody creates in sonorous space. The other two standard—bearers of local painting are the brothers Pietro and Ambrogio Lorenzetti, almost contemporaneous with Simone Martini and who perhaps both died during the plague of 1348. Their art has its roots in that of Duccio, of Giotto, of Giovanni Pisano, but, while in Pietro a prominant, powerful dramatic note resounds, Ambrogio's expressive key-board is rather varied, able to render the most subtle emotions.*
Noteworthy and great was the influence of all of these famous masters upon all paintings of the 1300's Stefano di Giovanni called "il Sassetta". delicious interpreter of late gothic taste but

also sensitive to the Renaissance insistance, Giovanni di Paolo who refreshed for the entire century the exquisities of the Siennese 1300's, stand out. Other valid painters of the 1400's emerging above an extraordinary group are, aside from the above mentioned Vecchietta, Bartolo di Fredi (who lived between the 13th and 14th century), Domenico di Bartolo, Matteo di Giovanni, Neroccio di Bartolomeo Landi and the before-mentioned Francesco di Giorgio Martini.

In the first half of the 1500's prominent are Domenico di Iacopo di Pace called "Mecarino" but known as "il Beccafumi" — very personalized in his violent palpitations of light and shadow — and the Vercellese Antonio Bazzi called "Sodoma", the most well-known of Italian leonardists. Two illustrious Umbrian painters, Perugino and even more, Pinturicchio, have left their signs on Siennese art. During these centuries the so-called minor arts also prospered at Sienna: in particular the goldsmith trade, wood-cutting, wrought iron, marble mosaics ("mixed-marble"), ceramics and, as real and true masterpieces, the miniature. After the fall of the Siennese republic the Medici family entered into the city government and, notwithstanding several sound initiatives, the foundation of Monte de' Paschi (1614) and the tutelage of the University, they were not able to arrest the general impoverishment of the economy and of the typical artiginal works of the region (silk, wool, leather, iron etc.). With the peace of Vienna, Tuscany passed, in 1738, to the Lorena among whom Pietro Lepoldo is well renowned. Governing from 1765 to 1790, he was protector of a political-agrarian, economic, tributary experiments, friend of the arts and innovator in the cultural field. After a Neopolitan parenthesis, during which Sienna was at the head of the Ombrone Department, included in the granduchy of Tuscany, the Lorena returned, following less reactionary politics in comparison with other sovreigns of the times. With the Italian Regeneration our city was ready to offer hospitality to those longing for that independence and liberty which was making itself felt in the entire Peninsula and, in 1859, she was the first of the Tuscan sisters to approve the union with the Italian Monarchy.

As for the arts, from the second half of the 1500's until the 1800's painting is still that which yields the major fruits. Among the many names, primary are those of the affable Francesco Vanni, the fertile fresco painter, Ventura Salimbeni, then — we are now into the first half of the 1600's — Rutilio Manetti, genial interpreter of the style of Caravaggio. At last, in the late 1600's and at the beginning of the 1700's, Giuseppe and Antonio Nasini acquire notoreity. Along with painting, other arts also contribute to the ulterior embellishment of Sienna without, however, modifying her most salient aspect; that of one of the most beautiful medieval cities in Italy.

Alphabetic Index

Itineraries

Itinerary I

St. Domenico Basilica - Sanctuary of St. Catherine - Branda Fountain - National Archeological Museum - Salimbeni Square - Church of Fontegiusta - Camollia Portal - St. Bernardino Oratory - St. Francesco Basilica - Tolomei Square - Church of the Holy Spirit - St. Martin's Church - University - Piccolomini Palace (State Archives) - Loggia della Mercanzia.

Itinerary II

Piazza del Campo - Public Palace - Civic Museum - Basilica of St. Mary of the Servi - Via di Città.

Itinerary III

Piazza del Duomo - Duomo - Museum of the metropolitan works - Baptistery - S. Maria della Scala hospital.

Itinerary IV

National Gallery - Church of S. Agostino.

Itinerary I

St. Domenico Basilica - Sanctuary of St. Catherine - Branda Fountain - National Archeological Museum - Salimbeni Square - Church of Fontegiusta - Camollia Portal - St. Bernardino Oratory - St. Francesco Basilica - Tolomei Square - Church of the Holy Spirit - St. Martin's Church - University - Piccolomini Palace (State Archives) - Loggia della Mercanzia.

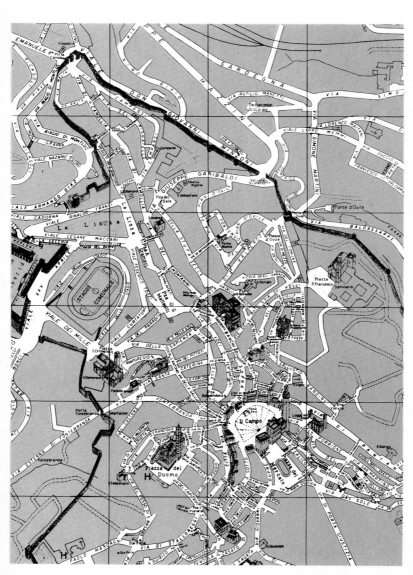

Let us begin our visit to Sienna from Piazza S. Domenico (St. Domenico Square) from where we can enjoy a stupendous view of the Cathedral, the Baptistry and the Torre del Mangia (tower of Mangia). The basilica of S. Domenico dominates the square.

BASILICA OF S. DOMENICO

A grandiose piece of architecture in brick of severe monastic gothic style, it was begun by the Domenicans who, from 1226 to 1254, constructed the rectangular nave and the roof with uncovered beams. After a pause, at the beginning of the 1300's, the temple was enlarged at the apse and crossway and below, a vast crypt was created. The pointed bell tower, erected in 1340, was lowered several times and finally refinished with battlements. Still in the 1300's the lateral chapels of the transept were erected and in 1400, the grandiose triumphal arch. After a fire in 1532, the church was burdened by baroque additions and, following the earthquake of 1779 reconsolidation was necessary. Recent restorations (1963) have restored to the church her antique aspect, enriched by the addition of stain-glass windows narrating the history of St. Catherine designed by Domenico Cantatore, Fabrizio Clerici, Giorgio Guaroni and Bruno Saetti. The entrance to the inside is found on the left side of the church.

Interior

Extremely grandiose is the form of the church, an Egyptian cross with one nave (T plan), square apse, chapels lateral to the presbitery, the ceiling with its uncovered beams, its high-coupled windows. We will limit ourselves to indicating only the most significant works.

At the end of the nave the Capella delle Volte (Chapel of Vaults, restored in 1952) opens up. It takes its name from the crossed vaults which close the bays and where a pilaster upon which traditionally, St. Catherine used to lean, stands. At the altar one finds a famous frescoe by Andrea Vanni, disciple of St. Catherine, which constitutes, by universal agreement, the only true portrait of St. Catherine. Among the other paintings of the chapel is the *Canonization of the Saint* by Mattia Pretti.

After the second altar on the right, is the aperture of St. Catherine's Chapel (1488) where the head of the Saint is custodized in a reliquary (1940). The chapel is renowned for it's frescoes by Sodoma — on the left of the altar, *Saint Catherine Fainting*; on the right, the *Exstasy of the Saint* — where the figures seem, as has often been said, to breathe. Still by Sodoma are *St. Catherine intercedes for the saving of the soul of the pleading Nicolò di Tuldo* (left wall) and *Sts. Luke and Girolamo* on the arch of the entrance portal (the *Blessed Raimondo* and *Tomaso Nacchi* are by Francesco Vanni).

Moreover, of particular artistic interest in the church are: the

1 - Basilica of St. Domenico - On the background the dome.

Sacred Vessel and the two marble *Angels* of the main altar by Benedetto da Maiano (1475 ca.); a *Madonna with Child and Saints* by Matteo di Giovanni (first chapel in the right transept); *St. Barbara on the throne between two Angels and Saints and above Epiphany* also by Matteo di Giovanni, and *Madonna with Child and four Saints*, and above *Pietà* by Benvenuto di Giovanni (second chapel in the left trasept), as well as a fragment of a fresco (*Madonna with Child, Saints and the Buyer*) by Pietro Lorenzetti (fourth altar on the left wall).   In the restored 3 naved crypt (beginning of the 1300's), a *Painted Cross* by Sano di Pietro, *Crucifixion and Saints* by Ventura Salimbebeni, and a wood panel by Sodoma (*The Eternal Father and Saints*) into which a small panel is inserted (*Madonna*) perhaps the work of Paolo di Giovanni Fei.

Upon leaving the church (in the remodelled 1400's cloister, frescoes by Lippi Memmi have recently been brought to light) one goes down the Via Camporegio and then, on the right, into the Costa di S. Antonio.   Here one finds the entrance into the Sanctuary of St. Catherine.

SANCTUARY OF ST. CATHERINE

It is a complex of buildings grouped around the house of Catherine Benincasa (1347-1380), indominate spirit both for her charitable acts towards the humble and suffering and in her political-religious activism, so much so as to contribute, with her passionate exhortations, to the return to Rome of Pope Gregory XI (1377) from his captivity at Avignon. Canonized in 1461 by Pope Pious II, and proclaimed Patron Saint of Italy (along with St. Francis) in 1939, her house and the family workshop (her father was a cloth dyer) were transformed beginning in 1465 (but the ornamentation was carried on into the 1700's) into a sanctuary, a famous goal for pilgrimages. From the Costa di S. Antonio we enter into the portico of the Counties of Italy (1941) and, in the precincts of a small, harmonious loggia (balcony) perhaps designed by Peruzzi, we approach the Church of the Crucifixion (ex-garden), named after the 1200's *Crucifix* (coming from the church of St. Catherine at Pisa) before which St. Catherine is said to have received the stigmata. The frescoes in the vault are by Giuseppe Nasini (late 1600's beginning 1700's), those on the walls by various 17th and 18th century artists, the canvases on the altars and walls are by Nasini and the 18th century masters. On the altar on the left is the *Deification of St. Catherine before Gregory XI* by Sebastiano Conca.

Opposite the entrance to the High Oratory (ex-kitchen), with majolica floors (usually covered) of the 1600's and compartmented ceiling restored by Riccio (1594), with an altarpiece by Fungai

(*Stigmata of St. Catherine* and with various paintings by Riccio. On the walls, above each of the 17 Renaissance stalls, are various paintings by Siennese artists of the XVI-XVIIth centuries, among which, a *Canonization of the Saint* by Francesco Vanni and the eloquent rievocation of the *Saint who, from St. Domenico's column, sees Jesus*, by Rutilio Manetti. One goes down from the oratory into a room (ex-bedroom of the Saint) with a gilded compartmented ceiling and walls frescoed by Alessandro Franchi (1896) and, on the

2

2 - *St. Domenico's - Andrea Vanni,* Portrait of St. Catherine.

altar, the *Saint receives the Stigmata* by Girolamo di Benevento; in the adjacent cell are some of St. Catherine's personal objects. One can descend still into the lower oratory (founded by the Benincasa family) or Church of St. Catherine in Fontebranda, today oratory of the city-section dell'Oca (of the goose, 1464-72), with frescoes by Girolamo del Pacchia and by Sodoma (note the gracefulness of the five *Angels*), paintings by Vincenzo Tamagni and Ventura Salimbeni and, on the altar, an expressive statue in painted wood with the figure

3

3 - St. Domenico's - *Il Sodoma,* Faint of St. Catherine.

13

of St. Catherine by Neroccio di Bartolomeo (1471).

Leaving the Sanctuary of St. Catherine (on the threshold of the house in the Tiratoio alley, one finds the following inscription in latin: "House of Catherine, bride of Christ") one descends into Via St. Catherine passing in front of the facades of the city-section of the Goose's seat and the Church of St. Catherine in Fontebranda (1474). Via della Galluzza, surmounted by 8 arched vaults and famous for its genuine medieval aspect, branches off from Via St. Catherine. At the end of Via St. Catherine the FONTE BRANDA (Branda Fountain) begins, already known of in 1081, amplified in 1188, and renovated by Giovanni di Stefano in 1446. Its aspect is that of a gothic palace or, better still, fort, so imposing is it: and one understands why upon the realization that the public fountains of Sienna were preciously protected due to the scarsity of water. Stupendous from here is the view of gigantic S. Domenico. Returning to St. Catherine's Sanctuary we again take the Costa di S. Antonio turning right into Via della Sapienza (road of knowledge) where, at n° 5 the Biblioteca degle Intronati (Library of the Stunned - 200,000 volumes and booklets, 1000 incunabula, 6000 manuscripts) stands, beginning with the collection of the archdeacon Sallustio Bendini (1759) and henceforth growing. One can view several of the most precious works with special permission. In Via della Sapienza n° 3 stands the National Archeological Museum.

NATIONAL ARCHEOLOGICAL MUSEUM

Founded in 1959, it is the fruit of the aggregation of various private collections, enriched by the findings of recent excavations in the Siennese region. It holds articles from prehistoric and Roman times coming from various localities and, principally from Monte Amiata, Pitigliano, Cetona, Castel del Piano, Chiusi, Chianciano, Pienza, Monteriffioni. The first room is dedicated to prehistoric objects (arms, utensils, burial relics) from the stone to the bronze and iron age, that is, up until protohistory. Rooms 2-10 (topographic section) house works from the Etruscan and Roman periods (VIIth cent. B.C. - IIIrd cent. A.C.) which evidence the particular versatility of the Etruscan civilization in assimilating and interpreting within their own spirit—completely realistically—motifs and elements drawn from other civilizations. Typical of the Etruscans are articles in "buchero" (black clay) and funeral vases depicting a human head in the upper part evoking the deceased (canopi) whose remains are contained in the lower part

4 - *St. Domenico's - Il Sodoma,*
Ecstasy of St. Catherine.

5 - *St. Domenico's - Il Sodoma,* St. Catherine Intercedes for the salvation of Niccolo's di Tuldo's Soul.

7 - *Outside of St. Catherine's Sanctuary.*

6 - *Sanctuary of St. Catherine - Portico of the Commons.*

8 - Fontebranda

of the vase. From the rich collection—which merits more ample space—we limit ourselves to indicating several of the more precious "pieces".

Room 5: Marble Sarcophagus with *Scenes from a lion hunt*, Roman art of the IIIrd cent. A.C.; "Sarcophagus of the Muse Chigi" (late Roman copy of a Greek exemplary of the IVth cent. B.C.). Room 7:

Head of an unknown personage (perhaps *Seneca*), Roman copy of a Helleniatic original found at Sienna; amphora with black figures representing a *Warrior on a chariot and a procession to Dionysis* (IVth cent. B.C.). Room 11 holds a collection of Etruscan coins from Piceno, Umbria, Lazio and Rome up until the end of the IInd cent. A.C. From the Museum we continue down Via della Sapienza where we find the 17th century church of S. Pellegrino della Sapienza, rising from where an antique chapel once stood, with internal baroque decorations rendered precious by a 13th century tabernacle in ivory and wood with incorporated sections of a 13th century altarpiece. Continuing down Via della Sapienza and going beyond the Costa dell'Incrociata, we find ourselves in Piazza Salimbeni, which is among the most characteristic squares in Sienna, fenced in on three sides by monumental Palazzo Spannocchi, projected by Giuliano da Maino (1470, completed in 1880 by Giuseppe Partini) of clear Florentine inspiration in its ornaments of smooth masonry spacious with two series of double windows with intervals of scored frames. At the end of the square stands the Salimbeni Palace, founded in the 13th century but restored and enlarged by Giuseppe Partini in 1879. It is a prime example of gothic architecture with its central section divided by elegant threefold windows enclosed by semiacute arches (on the inside, the historic archives and famous art works). On the left, the Tantucci Palace, Renaissance, designed by Riccio (1548). The Monte dei Paschi di Siena, one of the oldest Italian credit institutions (1624) and praiseworthy benefactor of cultural initiatives, is situated here. From Piazza Salimbeni, he who has time can reach the Camollia Portal. One must take Via Montanini, at the start of which is the Oratory of S. Maria delle Nevi (St. Mary of the Snows), perhaps designed by Francesco di Giorgio Martini, 1471, and embellished on the inside by one of the most touching paintings by Matteo di Giovanni, *The Madonna of the Snows*, 1471.

Digression
Beside the Oratory of St. Maria delle Nevi, walking up the Rustichette alley, we emerge in the Giacomo Matteotti Square where the small church of St. Catherine of the Drago city-section (bust of *St. Catherine* by Marrina) stands. From here we pass on into Piazza Antonio Gramsci and the "Lizza" where we can admire the 16th century church of S. Stefano della Lizza, adorned with a lovely *Visitation*

by Rutilio Manetti and with a *Madonna with Child* and *Saints*, a large polityptic by Andrea Vanni, 1400, with an altar stool by Giovanni di Paolo. From the "Lizza" one enters the Santa Barbara enclosure, also known as the Medici fort as Cosimo I de' Medici (1560) had it buit as a defence against external and internal enemies.
It is an imposing brick-walled military building. Today the Italian wine library lies within its walls, a permanent exhibition of Italian vintage wines. After leaving the fort and crossing the "Lizza" and via Sasso S. Bernardino we reach via Montanini.

End of digression

Facing via Montanini are ancient palaces and the Chiesa di S. Andrea, built by the Romans then restored in the 18th century and decorated internally with a 1445 polyptych attributed to Giovanni di Paolo. At the end of via Montanini, entering via Garibaldi from the right, we reach Chiesa della Compagnia di S. Sebastiano, a 17th century reconstruction of a very old building, with a clearly baroque interior, with frescoes by Rutilio Manetti and others, dedicated to the *life of S. Sebastiano*, a *crucifix* in wood which belonged to S. Bernardino, a copy of the *company gonfalon*, of Sodomic origin, and of heads of a coffin, attributed to Gerolamo del Pacchia.
Returning to via Montanini and proceeding a short way, we enter via Camollia. Behind the medieval Chiesa di S. Bartolomeo, belonging to the Porcupine Quarter, we pass beneath the arch of Fontegiusta. Making a slight deviation from here we can reach via Fontegiusta and finally the Church of Fontegiusta.

CHURCH OF FONTEGIUSTA

It was designed by Francesco Fedeli and Giacomo di Giovanni and was built between 1482 and 1484. Its facade is in Renaissance style brick and its portals have marble frames decorated by Urbano da Cortona, 1489, to whom is ascribed, though with some doubts, the reliefs above.
The interior has a square plan, divided into 3 naves by 4 columns and covered by cross-vaults. It is adorned with famous art works by Guidoccio Cozzarelli, Francesco Vanni, Girolamo di Benvenuto, Giovanni delle Bombarde, Baldassarre Peruzzi (fresco representing the *Sibyl who announced the birth of the Redeemer to Augustus*, 1528 ca.) and it possesses a marble tabernacle elegantly wrought by Mar-

9 - *Via della Galluzza.*

rina and Michele Cioli (begun in the 15th century) including a 14th century fresco (*Madonna and Child*).

Returning to Via Camollia, we pass the Church of S. Pietro alla Magione, of antique origin and renewed in 1942 (in the interior remain 13th century monochromatic frescoes and a *Madonna and Child* attributed to Riccio), and the house facing it by Baldissare Peruzzi

10 - Piazza Salimbeni (Salimbeni Square).

in order to reach the Camollia Portal, on the road to Florence. Constructed in the 13th century, it was renewed in 1604 using designs by Casolani. On the portal is inscribed in latin this hospitable welcome to the city: "Sienna opens its heart, even wider than this door, to you".

A short way off, in Via Vittorio Emanuele, a column stands in remembrance of the encounter between Federico III and Eleonora

10

of Portugal, in the presence of Enea Silvio Piccolomini (1452), this encounter is illustrated in a painting by Pinturicchio in the Piccolomini library of the Duomo. A little yay ahead is the antiportal of Camollia, that is, the first walled defense facing Florence, constituted of an aperture with embattlements overhead.

Let us now return to Piazza Salimbeni from where we go, with various digressions, towards the Piazza del Campo. From the

Oratory of S. Maria delle Nevi one descends into Via Vallerozzi, going up into Via dell'Abbadia to reach the Piazza Dell'Abbadia were we find the magnificent posterior facade (restored) in brick, of Palazzo Salimbeni. Facing this is the Church of S. Donato, begun around 1120 but almost completely rebuilt in the late 16th century and at the beginning of the past century: of antique it conserves the restored facade (with an elegant rose window in marble) and the inferior part of the apse. In the single-naved interior, the tiburium is antique while the decorative elements are, mostly, of Siennese artists of the XVII-XVIIIth centuries excepting a fresco by Luca di Tommè and several remains of 13th century Siennese frescoes.

One continues along Via dell'Abbadia taking a left down turn into Via dei Rossi. After passing the S. Francesco arch we come into Piazza S. Francesco where the ex-convent, the Basilica of S. Francesco and the Oratory of S. Bernardino are situated.

ORATORY OF S. BERNARDINO

It was built in the 14th century in homage to the Saint (Bernardino Albizzeschi, 1380-1440), in the same place where he used to draw a crowd with his sermons, of famous eloquence, based on the life, customs and history of his times. It consists of two overlaying oratories. Most significant artistically, is the Superior with walls and ceiling in wood decorated by Ventura Turapilli (1496) and, among the divisions of the pilasters, with magnificent frescoes by Sodoma, Beccafumi and Girolamo del Pacchia (1518-32), dedicated to the *Life of the Virgin and Saints* (excellent that of St. Francis by Sodoma). From the vestibule (the standard is painted by Francesco Vanni and the reliefs are by Giovanni di Agostino, 1341) one descends into the lower oratory with 17th century paintings, altarpiece by Brescianino and terracotta statues painted white (*S. Bernardino and St. Catherine*) by a 15th century master.

In the square rises the ex-convent of the church of S. Francesco; built in the 14th century, enlarged in 1518, and today seat of several University faculties. Particularly harmonious is the Renaissance cloister with ground floor porticoes within which the gothic doorway attributed to Domenico D'Agostino, originally adorned with frescoes by Ambrogio Lorenzetti judged by Ghiberti to be of supreme beauty, opens us. From the portico a stairway leads to the Basilica of S. Francesco.

BASILICA OF S. FRANCESCO

Here, where a small temple stood, in 1326 an enlargement was begun not terminated until 1475. Originally conceived in gothic form, the new church was added in the baroque epoque after a fire (1655). It was again renewed towards the end of the 18th century. The bell tower dates back to 1765; the facade was redone between 1894 and 1913; the two sides were lightened by high and narrow double windows with acute arches.

Interior

Along with S. Domenico, it is a typical example of gothic monastic architecture with a T plan and only one immense base nave, with chapels flanking the presbitery and a beamed roof. The whole is immersed in an irridescent light filtered through the double stain-glass windows and the four-arched nave windows. We will indicate only the works of particular excellence.

The Back facade: on the sides, the remains of Salimbeni tombs, of the XIVth cent. (on the right) and XIIIth century (on the left).

Right wall: fresco by Martino di Bartolomeo depicting the *Visitation and Saints* (first lunette) and frescoes by the 13th century Siennese School (first large niche of the small chapel). Behind the lateral portal, lies the tomb of the Tolomei, then on the floor, a tombstone legendarly presumed to be that of Pia de' Tolomei (cited by Dante).

Right transept: tomb of Cristoforo Felici di Urbano by Cortona, 1462 (second chapel to the right of the presbitery); *Madonna with Child*, by Andrea Vanni (first chapel).

Left transept: *Crucifix,* remains of a fresco by Pietro Lorenzetti (c. 1331), a piece of the most poignant tragic poetry (first chapel to the left of the presbitery). Third chapel to the left of the presbitery: right wall, *S. Lodovico d'Angiò at the feet of Boniface VIII*, remains of a fresco by Ambrogio Lorenzetti (c. 1331): scenes rich with color (in those parts not faded) with portrait studies of the personages; left wall, *Martyrdom of six francescan monks at Ceuta*, also by Ambrogio, a badly faded fresco. In the chapel of the wall opposite the transept, the pavement is of graffito by Lorenzo Marrina (1504) to a design by Lorenzo Pacchiarotti.

Upon leaving S. Francesco, one again passes under the archway of S. Francesco and then turns left in Via dei Baroncelli, and then right in Via del Giglio where the church of S. Pietro Ovile, of antique origin but reconstructed in 1753 and renewed in 1959, stands. In the interior is a fine copy of the *Annunciation* by Simone Martini, now in the Uffizi of Florence, perhaps executed by Matteo di Giovani; a noteworthy *Madonna with Child*, by "the master of S. Pietro Ovile" (XIVth cent.), works by Domenico di Niccolò de' Cori, by Giovanni di Paolo, and the remains of 13th century Siennese frescoes. Going down Via del Giglio and then left down Via del Moro, one arrives at the church of S. Maria di Provenzano, dedicated to a venerated relief image of the *Madonna* (XVth cent.), custodized in a rich tabernacle on the high altar which celebrates the miraculous apparition of the Virgin to Provenzan Salvani (see Palio). Also in this church, a fine *S. Cerbone* by Rutilio Manetti (1630) and several good 17th century sculptures.

After Via Moro, one reaches Piazza Tolomei (column with a *Female Wolf* in lead by Domenico Arrighetti, 1620) which starts, about half way down Via Banchi di Sopra, the "main street" of Sienna, always crowded (it connects the Loggia della Mercanzia with Piazza Salimbeni). In this square stands the PALAZZO TOLOMEI, 1205

11 - *Porta Camollia (Camollia Portal)*.

(perhaps the ground floor with three portals, of which the central, and largest, is enclosed in an ogival arch, was begun in this period) but restructured in 1265 and today headquarters of the Cassa di Risparmio of Florence which was responsible for its restoration. The facade is in stone with two rows of double windows surmounted by an acute arch englobing a small three-lobed rosette. Each floor lies upon a divisory frame marking the floor division; moulding is accentuated by a pronounced frame. In front of the palace stands the church of S. Cristoforo, of 13th century origin but restored in 1779. In the interior are various decorations, with works by Sano di Pietro (?), Bartolomeo Mazzuoli and Girolamo del Pacchia.

From Piazza Tolomei, going down Via Cecco Angiolieri (at n° 21/23 stands the house of the famous 13th century poet, who scoffed at the idealizations of the "sweet new style") we reach Via St. Vigilio, which takes its name from the ononymous church, whose interior is sumptuously decorated, with compartmented ceilings painted by Raffaele Vanni, paintings by Francesco Vanni, Volterrano and Mattia Preti, and sculptures attributed to Bernini and Algardi.

Almost facing the Church of S. Vigilio, on the other side of the short alleyway Castelliere, is a small square encircled by high walls, in cotto, of antique buildings called the "courtyard of the Ugurgieri Castle". It evokes, with live immediacy, medieval Sienna.

Returning to Via S. Vigilio and taking Via Sallusto Bandini, one of the most picturesque in Sienna, facing you, at n° 25, is the house of Bandini, a famous literary figure and economist (1677-1760). Going down Via Bandini we come into the small Virgilio Grassi square where the Church of St. Giovannino (or St. John the Baptist of the Staff) stands. It belongs to the XIVth century but was rebuilt in

12 - *Antiporta di Camollia.*

1563 and restored in 1876, in the city-section of Leocorno, it is pleasant and among other things, contains noteworthy paintings by Rutilio Manetti and Raffaele Vanni.

Continuing down Via di Follonica (at its opposite end lies the 16th century Follonica fountain with three arches with acute arcs), we reach Via di Pananeto: on the left is the church of S. Giorgio, of 12th century origin but rebuilt in 1741 (the bell tower is still romanesque), with paintings by Francesco Vanni and Sebastiano Conca. Proceeding into Via dei Pispini (exactly opposite, beyond the late XVIIth cent. Church of S. Gaetano, in the Nicchio section, is the Pispini Porta, 1326, with a lovely *Glory of the Angels*, the remains of a fresco by Sodoma) we enter the piazza S. Spirito where, in front of the graceful fountain of the Pispini, of 1534, the massive brick Church of S. Spirito arises.

CHURCH OF S. SPIRITO

Founded in 1498, its stone portal is dated 1519, perhaps designed by Peruzzi, and its cupola dated 1508 planned, apparently, by Cozzarelli. The interior, with one nave and a cupola at the intersection with the transept, is rich in art works, particularly Siennese workes of the XIV-XVIIth centuries; to be admired are, in the first chapel on the right with frescoes and an altarpiece by Sodoma, a *Manger Scene* in colored terracotta, partially by Ambrogio della Robbia (1504) and, in the third chapel on the left, two statues in wood by Giacomo Cozzarelli or Ambrogio della Robbia. Among the other masters who have adorned the church with their works, we may recall Beccafumi, Ventura Salimbeni, Manetti, Giuseppe Nasini, Girolamo del Pacchia, Sano di Pietro, Andrea Vanni, Cozzarelli, Balducci.

From the church of S. Spirito we return to Via di Pananeto which we follow to the right, taking an almost immediate left turn into Vicolo Magalotti which joins Via del Parrione. On the right, at n° 49, are the headquarters of the Archiconfraternity of Mercy, founded in 1260, with interior enriched by various works of the XIV-XVIth cent., among them two lovely statues by Marrina (*Risen Virgin* and *Archangel Gabriel*), of the early 15th century.

From here we continue into Via del Porrione shortly reaching the Piazzeta delle Logge del Papa. On the right rises the church of S. Martino.

CHURCH OF S. MARTINO

It was planned by the Siennese G. B. Pelori (1537); the facade, in late Renaissance style, is the work of the Ticinese Giovanni Fontana (1613).

The interior, a latin cross with one nave, a cupola and choir, abounds in marbles, decorations, works of art, with works by Guido Reni, del Guercino, the Tuscans Giovanni Antonio, Giuseppe and Annibale Mazzuoli, the Siennese Marrina (or by his workshop), Beccafumi, Raffaele Vanni, Giovanni di Lorenzo Cini. Of inestimable value are several remains of frescoes by followers of Pietro Lorenzetti (XIVth cent.) in the chapel to the left of the apse, and five statues in gilded wood in part by Iacopo della Quercia (*Madonna and Child*), in part by his school (4 Saints), on the third altar to the right.

Beside the Church of S. Martino stands the LOGGE DEL PAPA (Papal Lodgings) in three arches in the center, of a Renaissance Style. Its name derives from the fact that it was Pope Pio II Piccolomini who desired the lodging, Antonio Federighe who provided the plans (1462) and Francesco di Giorgio Martini who carried out the ornamentation.

From here we take the Via Banchi di Sotto arriving at the entrance to the UNIVERSITY, since 1915 situated in the 16th century ex-monastery of S. Virgilio. Today it houses the jurisprudence, medicine and farmacology departments and the Library of the juridical club, with over 400,000 booklets and volumes. In the particle is the monumental tomb of Niccolò Aringhieri da Casole (1374). The University of Sienna is among the oldest in Italy. It was probably founded by an exodus of professors and students from the University of Bologna and was already cited in 1240. Its most florid period

13 - Palazzo Tolomei

14 - Loggia della Mercanzia (Merchandise Loggia).

was in 13th and 14th century when it had among its masters Cino da Pistoia, il Panormita, il Filelfo. In recent times the Siennese anatomist and physiologist Paolo Mascagni (1752-1815) and the jurist Luigi Cremona (1748-1830), among others, have taught there.

In front of the university is the PALAZZO PICCOLOMINI, a splendid Renaissance building designed by Bernardo Rossellino and begun in 1469 by Pietro Paolo Porrina. Its facade is of smooth, embossed stone broken by two rows of windows with ornate frames. Since 1885 it has contained the STATE ARCHIVES, founded by the Lorena, an inestimabe collection of documents regarding the life of Sienna from the XIVth century till today. On view are some of the most precious memorials of personages named by Dante, deliberations of the Siennese republic, decrees and documents on various subjects among them the "caleffo" (i.e. the collection of documents approving the rights of the republic) said to be by Assunto, finely refinished in miniatures by Niccolò di Ser Sozzo Tegliacci, the "statute of merchandizing" miniatured by Sano di Pietro, Papal seals, saints manuscripts, personal objects of artists etc. The collection of small wooden panels documenting the "Biccherna", that is, the magistrature which handled (along with the "Gabella") Sienna's finances and superintended the execution of public works: these panels depict, without interruptions, the years 1258 to 1659. The camerlingoes (managers of the pontifical Court) were substituted every six months and, at the end of their mandate, they gathered together the most important documents to be translated on wooden panels by the most prestigious artists of the day: among these, the two Lorenzetti brothers, Giovanni di Paolo, Taddeo di Bartolo, Sano di Pietro, il Vecchietta and Francesco di Giorgio Martini, il Beccafumi.

At the end of Via Banchi, below, one arrives at a spot named "Croce del Travaglio" (Crossway of labor or trouble) where the upper Banchi, the lower Banchi and the Via di Città meet. The name originates from the clashes ("travaglio"-trouble), which often took place here, between the various citizen parties, so frequent that barriers had to be erected to separate the contendents.

Facing is the LOGGIA DELLA MERCANZIA composed of three arcades on the facade and one on the side. It was built in the first half of the 14th century and can already be considered a Renaissance structure graced by late gothic elements (the niches holding religious objects in the pilasters). Designed by Sano di Matteo (1417-29) but terminated by Pietro del Minella (1444), it contains statues of *Saints* by Vecchietta and Urbano da Cortona (1464), vaulted ceilings with stuccoes and frescoes from the mid 15th century, wrought iron railings

of the late 18th century, and its upper storey was added in the 16th century.

On the left of the loggia, is a house-tower at whose side stands a medieval palace adorned by a graceful three-fold window. From the loggia, by going down Vicolo S. Pietro, we soon come into Piazza del Campo.

Itinerary II

Piazza del Campo - Public Palace - Civic Museum - Basilica of St. Mary of the Servi - Via di Città.

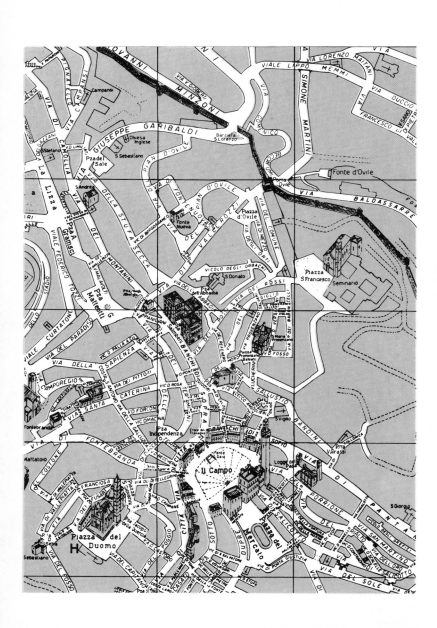

PIAZZA DEL CAMPO

During one of his visits to Sienna, in 1581, Montaigne noted in his "Trips Journal": "The Piazza (del Campo) of Sienna is the most beautiful in Italy". Like him, many other visitors, both foreign and Italian, have remained enthralled by the unmistakeable image of this square called "tout court" the Campo. Unconfoundable, above all, for its shell-like form, then for its sloping quality (in fact, from here arise the three hills upon which the city is built), and last, for its circle of decorous palaces with towers and embattlements faced by the soft curve of the Public Palace. Six centuries ago the Piazza began to take this form, evidencede by the central brick work, used for the first time in 1374, and divided into nine sections by stripes of light colored stone. Sections which evoke a memory—even more evoked in the inside of the Public Palace—that of the government of the Nine. For all these centuries the Campo has been the center of public life in Sienna: here its population gathered together in the happy and sad hours of the republic, here it faced factions avid for supremacy, here the most famous of ther priests admonished the people and the powerful—best known of all is San Bernardino—here, lastly, times of anguish preceding the surrender of Sienna to the troops of Medeghino sent by Carlo V of Spain, were lived. But the Campo—almost superfluous to say—is today above all famous for its horse race, the Palio, which we will discuss later.

Within the architectonic frame of the square, the FONTE GAIA (Gay fountain) is harmoniously inserted. Here one finds free copies (done by Tito Sarrocchi in 1868) of the original sculptures by Iacopo della Quercia, now sadly worn (see Public Palace). The bas reliefs represent, from left to right: the *Creation of Adam, Knowledge, Hope, Force, Prudence, Madonna and Child between two Angels, Justice, Charity, Temperance, Faith, The Expulsion of Adam and Eve from the Garden of Paradise*. The water in the bowl is alimented by jets from two *Siennese Wolves* and *Protomes*. The fountain took its name from the festivities which took place in 1300 at the first spurts of water flowing into Piazza del Campo due to the construction of an aqueduct 23 kilometers long.

15 - *Piazza del Campo*

THE PUBLIC PALACE - FACADE

From here the facade of the Public Palace transplays all its elegance and splendor of one of the most celebrated gothic constructions in Italy. Built between 1297 and 1310, perhaps on a design by Agostino di Giovanni and Angelo di Ventura, it then contained the central part which rises towerlike above the two lateral wings which have three-fold windows on first and second floors up to the height of the blind arches which are still today visible. From 1327 it was enlarged to include, on the right flank, the prisons, then (1330-42) the council room of the "Campana" (bell). In 1690-81 the third floor of three-fold windows was added. The original facade of the Public Palace served as model for many successive 13th and 14th century Siennese palaces. Coexisting within its structures are the typical elements of Siennese gothic: the acute arch including arches of lowered intersections ("Siennese arch") which frames the doors and windows of the first storey; the use of travertine in the lower zone and terracotta above; but particularly "that timidity of projection which marks the linear shadows, almost calligraphic, on the surface of the walls" (Gino Chierici). Upon the spandrels of the doors and windows the symbol of Sienna continually recurs as motif - "la Balzana", distinct on a black and white background. The heights of the palace are crowned with embattlements, today no more than simple decorative elements underlining the gothic verticality of the architecture. The two extremes of the central tower are surmounted by now empty bell chambers. The right hand chamber is the oldest; the adjacent one was added in the 17th century. On the last floor of the tower the symbol of San Bernardino of Sienna appears: a large copper disc with the monogram of Christ, painted in 1425 by Battista di Niccolò of Pavia; at the corners, two stone wolves. The coat of arms of the Medici, at the center of the three-fold window on the second floor was added in 1560, after their conquest of Sienna.

From the left angle the TORRE (tower) DEL MANGIA rises, agile and elegant, a shaft of red stone topped by a crowning ornament by Lippo Memmi, Simone Martini's brother-in-law, idealized in 1341, "in a moment of ecstatic inspiration" (Chierici). The shaft of the tower, 88 meters high, was built between 1338 and 1348 by the brothers Minuccio and Francesco di Rinaldo da Perugia; the ornamentation, which reaches, including the lightening rod, a height of 102 meters, was carried out (it said using Memmi's project) by Ago-

16 - Il Campo - Fonte Gaia.

stino di Giovanni. The bell chamber, situated halfway up the top ornamentation, holds a large bell, cast in 1666, called "Campanone" (big bell) or "Sunta", a Siennese abbreviation of the Assumption of the Virgin to which Sienna made a votive pledge before the battle of Monteaperti. The appellative of "Mangia" given to the tower derives from Mangiaguadagni, the nickname of a certain Giovanni di Duccio, to whom initially the task of sounding the hours was given and who has since become legendary (see Beyond). Later, until 1780, an automon was used still called "Mangia". The first tower clock, produced by a certain Maestro Perino, was installed in 1360 but was substituted 60 years later with another realized by the Jesuit Giovanni da Milano.

Under the Torre del Mangia, beside the Public Palace, is the CAPEL-LA DI PIAZZA (The chapel), erected by the Siennese as the disso-lution of a votive pledge made during the plague of 1348. Originally (1352-76) Domenico di Agostino and then Giovanni di Cecco erected only pilasters covered by a roof. Around a century later, from

17 - Palazzo pubblico (Public Palace).

1463 to 1468, Antonio Federigni gave it a more monumental aspect, adding Renaissance arches and a new facade. The statues of the *Saints* found in the pilaster niches were done by Mariano di Angelo and Bernardino di Tommè, excepting the St. Bartholomew, in the left lower pilaster, modelled by Lando di Stefano. 12th century marbles with bas reliefs in the Pisano style, surround the sides of the chapel, others, by Enea Becheroni (1848) enclose the front. Of the 13th century are the gates in wrought iron by Pietruccio di Betto and Conte di Lello Orlandi. In ancient times daily masses were celebrated in the chapel and for the *Sanctus*, as Montaigne recalls, a trumpet was sounded to call the devout to prayer.

From one of the doors on the side of the Cappella di Piazza, one enters the CORTILE DEL PODESTÀ, (Courtyard of the Mayor), created around 1325 and recently well restored. Rising from here like a Dolomitic spire is the Torre del Mangia (Mangia Tower), towering above the brick structures of the courtyard, ingraciated by three-fold ogival windows and underneath by a portacle. The walls hold coats of arms of the ancient governors of the city. Near one of these is the mutilated statue of Mangia which was somewhat like the statue of Pasquino at Rome, against whom all sorts of funny volgarities were launched. On the back of the statue are (barely visible) 13th century frescoes. Those with strong legs can brave the stairs (332 steps) which lead to the castle of the bell tower from where they can enjoy a splendid view of Sienna's hills and towards the south, of Siennese Montagnola and Mount Amiata. From the courtyard is an access to the TEATRO COMUNALE DEI RINNOVATI (Communal Theater of the Renewed), originally the hall of the Grand Council of the Republic, adapted for use as a theater by the siennese Bartolomeo Neroni, called "il Riccio" (1560), but rebuilt after a fire, by the famous Antonio Galli called "il Bibiena" (1753). Careful restorations were carried out in 1951.

Interior

The entrance to the Public Palace is from the portal on the right, beautified by a frieze of leaves surmounted by a statue near which a column bearing a copy of the *Female Wolf* by Giovanni and Lorenzo di Turino, in gilded lead, stands. We will see the original shortly. One enters the atrium where two bronze armlets with bells by Giacomo Cozzarelli coming from the Palazzo del Magnifico (see intinerary 3) are on display. From the atrium one passes into a vestibule divided into four bays on whose walls are placed two *Wolves* in stone and pipes (ornamental motifs) perhaps by Giovanni Pisano or by his school (XIVth cent.) flanking a small statue of *Moses* by Federighi. On the right wall of the third bay, a fresco by Sano di Pietro from 1446, an effigy of *Pietro Alessandrino and the Blessed Siennese Ambrogio Sansedoni and Andrea Gallerani.*

The rooms at the sides of the vestibule are offices and therefore not usually open to visitors (only with special permission). They, too, are decorated with pictoral and plastic works and contain, among other things, one of the most scenographic compositions of Sano di Pietro (*Incoronation of the Virgin and Saints*, 1445 in the Biccherna room), as well as paintings by Vecchietta, Siennese masters of the 13th and 14th century and, in particular, of Sodoma (XVIth cent.) of whom a mediated and vibrant *Resurrection* (1535) excells, ornamenting the room of the general secretary.

CIVIC MUSEUM

From the entrance one goes up to the second floor. In the vestibule are; the original of the *Female Wolf* by Giovanni di Turino (1429-30) whose copy we have seen at the entrance to the Palace, and a *Madonna and Child*, precious fragment of a *Maestà* by Ambrogio Lorenzetti (1340).

Tre Globe room

The name of this room derives from a map painted by Ambrogio Lorenzetti which has since disappeared.

Left wall: It is occupied by a very celebrated frescoe of the *Maestà* (Madonna with Child enthroned, adored as sovreign of the world) by Simone Martini. This fresco is among the first works by the famous Master, dated 1315, and restored in the central part by Martini himself in 1321. Posterior to the *Maestà* of Duccio di Buoninsegna by only 4 years (see Museum dell'Opera of the Cathedral), this fresco of Martini stands out for its more liberal compositional conception (the confrontation is valid only with the *recto* of Duccio's altarpiece) "the movement seems studied to lend relief to the musical continuity of their profiles and the exceedingly refined rhythms of their preciously ornated garments" (Carli), and for the atmosphere in which the scene is represented which is no longer the divinized gold of the Byzantines but a sky glue. What is more, the Madonna doesn't

18 - Palazzo pubblico - Cortile del Podestà (Podestà Courtyard) and Torre del Mangia.

appear, as in Duccio, only as an ecclesiastical symbol of transcendence, but also as the figure of mother of humanity, the sweet consoler of the afflicted: "My dilect, remember", reads, in fact, the inscription underneath, "He among you who honestly prays—as you wish, I will content you". The Virgin sits on an ornate gothic throne with Christ Child in the act of blessing on her lap, under a silk canopy carressed by a breeze whose pennons are sustained by the apostles. These, together with the saints—among whom are the four protectors of Sienna: Ansano, Vittore, Savino and Crescenzio, and two angels bearing cups of flowers, crown her in an act of choral homage. The frescoe has suffered in the past and suffers yet from the insidious dampness which has damaged its chromatic substances; studies to preserve it from ulterior damage are being carried out.

Above the arches are two frescoes in yellow earth: on the right, the *Victory of the Siennese over the Florentines at Poggio Imperiale* (near Poggibonsi), by Giovanni di Cristoforo and Francesco d'Andrea (1480); on the left, the *Victory of Siennese over the English company of Cappello at Sinalunga*, by Lippo Vanni (1370). Other frescoes decorate the pilasters: from the right, the *Blessed Siennese Andrea Gallerani and Ambrogio Sansedoni*, work by a 16th century master, then a *St. Catherine* by Lorenzo di Pietro called "il *Vecchietta*" (1461), depictions of the Saint after which she was raised to the honors of the altar: one notices the plasticity of the image against background of a decorative Renaissance apse. Following are the figures of *S. Bernardino*, by Sano di Pietro (1450) and the *Blessed Bernardo Tolomei* by Sodoma (1553).

On the adjacent wall, above, is another masterpiece by Simone Martini (1329): the fresco depicting GUIDO RICCIO DA FOGLIANO. The composition evokes Guido Riccio, adventurer-captain of the Siennese, while he rides ahead to assault the castle of Montemassi. This theme is quite different from that of the *Maestà*: in the latter, a sacred image, in Guido Riccio, a profane, military theme: but both are equal in the poetic intensity of their composition. The crowd of images in the Maestà is substituted here by one group, that of the horse and rider which "seem gigantic against the background of the horizon like a metaphysical mask two busts; and the horse's eye looks out from his black and yellow draperies like the eye of a monster" (Emilio Cecchi). A heraldic group, this, so efficaciously represented as to seem the symbol of the medieval military world, or else the soldier who, having abandoned all the pleasures

19 - *Palazzo pubblico - Cappella di Piazza (The Chapel of the Square).*

20 - *Palazzo pubblico - Simone Martini*, Guido Riccio da Fogliano.

of life, turns, solitary, to explore the paths of death. Simone, with superb synthesis, has also given life to an unforgettable countryside: two hills defended by trenches and topped by the two castles to be conquered (Montemassi and Sassoforte, in Maremma) and, on the extreme right of the fresco, another higher and steeper hill from which the militia, steeling themselves for battle, sallies forth.

Underneath this fresco is a large wooden panel by Guido da Sienna depicting the *Madonna and Child enthroned*, dating 1221 and coming from S. Domenico where for many centuries it remained as an object proof of the priority of the Siennese school over the florentine one. Today this problem has been overcome (even apart from this work) since the date is universally judged to be inexact or, rather, perhaps altered during restorations in the first part of the 13th century by a

20

scholar of Duccio. According to prevalent opinions, in fact, the work schould be backdated almost half a century, particularly in consideration of stylistic qualities. Besides Guido da Sienna's *Madonna* are two splendid and grandiose figures of Saints by Sodoma (1529): *S. Vittore and S. Ansano baptizing.*

Room of Peace

This was the public seat of the government of the nine already mentioned. Lasting from 1292 to 1355, this government signalled the downfall of the ghibellines and the prevalence of the florentine-favored guelfs at Sienna. To a relative political stability strenuously defended by the nine—representatives of the rich borgoisie and of high finance within an articulated organism of ministries, effectively regulating the life of the republic—, to a change to higher economic conditions, corresponds an indiscutable cultural progress (particularly concerning the protection of the university) and an incomparable flourishing of the arts.

It is to this government of the Nine that Ambrogio Lorenzetti dedicated the grandiose frescoes (1338-40) which constitute the vastest complex of medieval painting dedicated to a profane subject. Ambrogio affronted the theme of the glorification of this government using cycles of allegories in which abstract concepts (government, virtues, vices etc.) are clothed, as is usual, in human vestiges. And it is retained probable that for this complex chain of figures, commented by long explicative didactics in common language, Ambrogio had to consult scholars and philosophers of probable aristotolic extraction.

Wall opposite the window: *Good Government*. The conception is that the government of the Nine (symbolized by the king enthroned with a black and white garment, the colors of Sienna, colors recurrent also in the twins and on the wolf) is good because it is based upon the observation of human and divine virtues. The human virtues are personified by the six women sitting beside the king: on his right, *Peace, Force, Prudence*; on his left, *Magnaminity, Temperance, Justice*. The divine virtues—*Faith, Hope, Charity*—hover around the king's head. The highest virtue of the government is, however, *Justice*, depicted a second time by the gentle-woman seated, isolated, at the extreme left-hand side of the scene, who is in turn inspired by knowledge who watches over her. In this way all sects of citizens are concordant in rendering homage to the government: they are represented here by the 24 personages holding two cords (according to an etimological misinterpretation but more acceptable figuratively than the correct one, of the word "concordant" which means *with one's heart* and not *with cords*). These cords hang from the two plates of the scales of *Justice* over which two angels watch (symbols of Aristotle's commutative and distributative justice), they are drawn up by *Concord* (on whose knees lies a carpenter's plane destined to humiliate the pretentions of the ambitious) and passed by her to the 24 personages who, in turn, offer it to the king. Lastly, the military security of the government is exemplified on the right of the fresco by armed warriors who stand guard over a group of prisoners.

From this great and complex lucubration in all its medievalness, Ambrogio Lorenzetti arises triumphant due to the acuteness of his observations which give the personages depicted in the fresco—notwithstanding the sobriety of style in conformance with the times and the austerity of the theme—those moral and sentimental qualities which they were supposed to symbolize: in this sense, one sees in particular, the images of Peace (for whom this room is named), of Concord, of Prudence and the visages, some resigned, some suffering, of the prisoners of war.

The entrance wall: *The effects of a good government in the city and in the country*. This recounts how a good government renders a city both rich and prosperous, and this is illustrated by the quantity and decor of her buildings, by the luxuriant attire of her citizens, by their festive optimism, by the prosperity of their markets. In this, Ambrogio presents us with a vision, certoinly not completely arbitrary due to his constant attention to veracity—of the Sienna of his times, with its many house—towers, its alleys, its squares where young girls dance playing the tambourine, couples are married and commerce flourishes. This in the most scenographic fresco of the whole cycle, the most famous for its evocative immediacy and, at the same time, for the great variety of its images which allow us to settle our gaze upon a single point of observation, and lastly, for the festivity of color which the "chemistry of centuries" has unfortunately modified but not extinguished.

If the government is good, the countryside, too, feels the effects: thus Ambrogio evokes for us in the other large fresco on the wall, scenes beyond the walls of the city which act as divisory frames between the two compositions, the hilly region surrounding Sienna, so harsh and yet so tenaciously and geometrically ordered and cultivated (in the background a brief glance at Maremma: the port of Talamone): Also in this sadly faded fresco various anecdotes abound, delicious tales of country life: he who goes hunting with a falcon, he who pushes an ass or fat pig with his cane, he who reaps and thrashes grain, he who fishes, those going to market while the animals graze tranquilly or flee, frightened, before a hunter.

Opposite wall: *Bad government and its effects in the city and on the countryside*. These are the frescoes in worse repair in the whole room, so much so as to be deciphered with difficulty. They are, obviously—the opposite allegorically and also figuratively—of the

21 - Palazzo pubblico - Simone Martini, The Majesty.

concepts expressed in the previous frescoes: one passes, in synthesis, from good to evil. Thus the *Bad government* is enthroned with its sword of outrageousness and the chalice of intemperance posed at the feet of a black goat (Belzebu?): his eyes are crossed, his fangs are curved like the horns which sprout from his head. Above him are *Tyranny, Avarice and Empty Pride*, and by his side sits *Cruelty, Deceit, Fraud, Fury, Discord and Perfidy*; *Justice in chains*, mocked and oppressed. As for the *Effects of bad government*, the faded fragments of the fresco lead us to imagine the decay of a city in ruins and the desolation of a countryside infested with robbers, a dark kingdom of violence and death.

Room of Pilasters

From the left: *S. Bernardino preaching in the Field* and *S. Bernardino exorsizing an obsessed person*, diptych by Nerocchio di Bartolomeo Landi; the *Saints Stephan, Magdelan and Anthony*, triptych by the Siennese school at the end of the 13th century (Martino di Bartolomeo?), an *Annunciation* of the 13th century, a *Madonna and Child* - panel by a valid master in the school of Duccio. Under glass are precious testimonies of Siennese art and history of the 14th to 16th century. One returns to the Globe Room and from there passes into the antichapel.

Anti-chapel

The walls are frescoed by Taddeo di Bartolo (1407-14), a Siennese painter and illustrator, somewhat out of the linearistic traditions of local painting "because of his hard, outlined style" (Cecchi). These frescoes depict Allegories of Virtue and *Pagan divinities, Illustrious men of anique* Rome, of whom Sienna feels herself son. The wooden statue on the wall (St. Nicholas of Bari) is attributed to Federighi.

Chapel

The series of frescoes by Taddeo di Bartolo (1407) continues. In the vault, on the left wall, in the lunettes, they evoke Episodes of the life of the Virgin among which are the *Death* and the *Assumption*. The entrance to this chapel is constituted by an extremely delicate gate of leaded wrought iron designed in squares, each of which contains 9 quadrilobes, executed in 1437 by the Siennese Giacomo di Giovanni and by his son Giovanni. On the right, a small, hanging holy water vessel with the *Savior and Angels* in gilded bronze, by Giovanni di Torino (1434). Hanging in the chapel is a rare, gothic lamp sculpted by Cecco di Nanni del Ciucca and painted by Cristoforo da Cosona (1370). The finely worked altar by the Siennese Lorenzo di Mariano called "il Marrina" contains one of the most praised compositions of Soloma (*Sacred Family with S. Leonardo*, 1535 ca.) with an enchanting landscape in the background. On the right, under the arch, is an encased organ with splendid engravings by Giovanni di Pietro and Ghino d'Antonio (1524). Lining the walls are 21 COIR stalls with engraved backrests (*the articles of the Creed*), constituting the masterpiece of Siennese woodcutting. Domenico di Niccolò (1415-28), the author, has since been called "dei Cori" (of the choir) in honor of his marvellous work.

The Cardinal room

Above the entrance is a crucifix on a 13th century wood panel; at the pilaster, a tabernacle by Guidoccio Cozzarelli (or by Matteo di Giovanni); on the right wall, two stuccoed wooden statues (*Saints Ambrose and friar Anthony*) judged to be (with some doubts) by Antonio Federighi, and a fragment of a fresco perhaps by Ambrogio Lorenzetti (*three Saints and the commissioner*). Higher up, on this and the opposite walls, another fresco with *figures of Saints*, painted "ex-voto" by 13th and 14th century Siennese.

Consistory room

The entrance portal is elegantly in marbles and gildings by the Florentine Bernardo Gambarelli called "il Rossellino" (who was also architect); the engravings on the wooden doors are perhaps by Domenico di Niccolò. The frescoes decorating the vaults, illustrating *Episodes of Civic Virtue* are taken from Greek and Roman history. These frescoes are admirable works from Domenico Beccafumi's mature period (1529-35): to note is the radiance of color, the richness of shading, the majesty of the architectonic perspective (in the center of the vault *Justice, Brotherhood* and *Self-Respect* are depicted). Three large Gobelin tapestries of the 16th century (*Allegories of the Earth, Air and Fire*) and five smaller Florentine ones (more *Allegories*) adorn the walls; above the portal, the *Justice of Solomen* belived to be by Luca Bordano (XVIIth cent.). Retracing our steps, we then enter the Baglia room.

22 - *Palazzo pubblico - Sala del mappamondo (Globe's Hall).*

Room of the Balia or Priors

It was so called because it was the seat of the ministry of the Balia. Divided in two by an arch, it's walls are entirely covered with frescoes done in 1407 by Spinello Aretino and his son Parri. They illustrate, in 15 squares, the most important *Episodes in the life of Pope Alexander III*, the Siennese Rolando Bandinelli, Pope from 1159 to 1181, proud enemy of Barbarossa, allied with the Lombard Communities, founder of Alessandria, cruel repressor of the Catari. The work is interesting more for its documentation of customs,

activities, artisans of the times than for its esthetic qualities. In the vault of the room are *Allegories of 16 Virtues* by Martino di Bartolomeo (1408); the door on the right was carved by Domenico di Niccolò; the wooden bench is the work of Barna di Turino (1410).

Room of the Regeneration

The frescoes, by Siennese and Tuscan painters of the late 18th century narrate *Salient Episodes from the life of Vittorio Emanuele II*, from his encounter with Radetzky, after the unfortunate *Battle of Novara*,

23 - Palazzo pubblico - Ambrogio Lorenzetti, Effects of Good Government in Town.

and at the *Burial in the Pantheon.* Moreover: marble busts of political and artistic personalities of the last century, by Siennese sculptors, fill the room.

Collection of various arts

In the first room, Siennese ceramics and majolica wares of the 1400's, works by local artisans and many sketches and exemplars of the medieval weaving industry. On the walls, paintings by Siennese masters and by other schools. Particularly rich is the numismatic collection, housed in 4 rooms. It comprehends more than 6000 coins of Italian states with an almost total documentation of those coined in the Siennese republic, as well as precious esemplars from Populonia and a copious collection of Roman coins and seals. There are, moreover, over 1500 medals from the Renaissance epoque to today. The

walls are adorned with 14th and 15th century paintings. One goes up the large stairway, adorned by a *Madonna* by Neroccio di Bartolomeo (1481), and, after the first ascent, enters 3 rooms containing plaster casts of many of the principal works (among which the portal by Petronio at Bologna and the sepulchre of Ilaria del Carretto at Lucca) of the greatest Siennese sculptor, Iacopo della Quercia (1372?-1438). One then goes up into the Loggia.

Loggia

Here, along the walls, original sculptures in great part eroded by time and water, which Iacopo della Quercia executed for the FONTE GAIA in piazza del Campo, are displayed.

This piece was commissioned to Iacopo in 1414 but, due to various impediments, was only terminated in 1419. Note here the two statues which flanked the fountain (now missing at the actual fountain), that is, the figures of *Rea Silvia* (or *Charity*) and of *Acca Laurenzia* (on which the pupil Francesco di Valdambrino perhaps participated). The order of the statues is that of the Fonte nel Campo. So enthusiastic were the Siennese at the sight of the finished work that Iacopo gained the surname "of the fountain". Stylistically, this sculptural complex is collocated in the Master's late gothic Renaissance vision, stamped with his own, unconfoundable personality. This is expressed in the austere composure of the female faces—more heroines than women—accentuated and beautiful that of Rea Silvia, in which one feels a fleeting tenderness. The panorama from the loggia is stupendous. From here one has access to the grand hall of the Signoria.

Grand hall of the Signoria

It is now the room of the communal council, beautified by paintings of historical subjects of the Siennese Amos Cassioli (XIXth cent.) and works by local 15th century artisans. The successive rooms gather together an anthology of works, the greatest part of which refer to the history, life and customs of Sienna. Remarkable is the collection of prints, maps and images of illustrious Siennese, as well as documentation on the Palio. On the third floor of the palace (which will become an amplification of the museum) one can view a fresco by Sodoma (*Madonna with the Eternal Father and Saints*, 1539) located, originally, on the altar of the Square's Chapel.

The monumental palaces girding the Capo are many. Particularly outstanding because of its grandiosity is the curved, reddish PALAZZO SANSEDONI. In its origins, that is, in the first half of the 12th century, the building was much more modest. It was brought almost to its present proportions around 1339 by Agostino di Giovanni and collaborators. In those times its tower was much higher —almost as high as that of the Mangia—but it was lowered in 1760 so that only a stump remains. The interior, rich with art works, contains several rooms frescoed around the middle of the 17th century by the Florentine Gian Domenico Ferretti. Attached to Palazzo Sansedone is the Chigi Zondadari Palace, a 17th century elaboration of a more antique edifice. Continuing beyond Palazzo Sansedone past Vicoli S. Pietro, the back facade of the Loggia della Mercanzia appears, designed by Ferdinando Fuga (1763). On the other side of the square the palace-tower d'Elci (XVIth cent.) crowned by embattlements, rises. Going up Via Dupré we come into Piazza del Mercato

(Market Square) where can view the rear facade of the Public Palace.

From here one finds the entrance to several of her rooms (once used for storage of salt) now readapted to housing cultural exhibitions. On the left side of the square, going up a stairway, we come into Via Salicotto, with a splendid view of several parts of the city and the Church of S. Agostino; we pass the Oratory of S. Giacomo (1531) of the city—section of the Torre (tower). On the inside is the *Decapitation of S. Giacomo* and a *Crucifixion*, masterpieces by Manetti. Annexed to the oratory is the Museum (*Going to Calvary*, by Sodoma). At the end of the street we turn right into Via S. Girolamo, at the start of which is the Church of S. Girolamo with its rich interior, embellished with, among other things, works by Cozzarelli, Sano di Pietro and Giuliano da Firenze. One continues down Via dei Servi at the end of which, in Piazza Alessandro Manzoni — from where we have a splendid view of the Duomo — the Basilica of S. Maria die Servi stands.

THE BASILICA OF SANTA MARIA DEI SERVI

Built in 1200, and enlarged between 1473 and 1523, the façade remains unfinished. On its right an impressive Romanesque bell tower is lightened by windows which gradually widen from single openings at the bottom to four at the top. The whole architectural complex, in brick, was restored in 1926.

Interior

The exterior gives no hint of the harmonious elegance of the interior, with the three longitudinal aisles in pure Renaissance style (designed by Peruzzi or Porrina and carried out by Ventura Turapilli) separated by a double marble colonnade (1471-1528), and with transept and apse still in late Gothic style. The basilica is embellished by many works of art painted between the 13th and 16th centuries by Siennese artists (Rutilio Manetti, Francesco Vanni, Segna di Bonavetura, Girolamo del Pacchia, Giacomo Cozzarelli, Bernardino Fungai, Giovanni di Paolo, Taddeo di Barolo, Giacomo di Mino del Pellicciaio). We mention here only the more eminent artistically. First column onthe right: it is next to a beautiful holy water stoup, part of which comes from the end of 1200.

The second altar in the right aisle: *Madonna and Child with two angels* known as *Madonna del Bordone*, signed by Coppo di Marco-

24 - *Palazzo pubblico - The Chapel.*

24

valdo and dated 1261, later partly repainted by a pupil of Duccio and recently restored: this is the work, still associated with the detail of Byzantinism, that the Florentine, Coppo di Marcovaldo, taken prisoner by the Siennese at the battle of Monteaperti, painted to secure his release from prison.

Third altar in the right aisle: *Nativity of Mary*, a grandiose composition by Rutilio Manetti. Fifth altar of the right hand aisle: *Slaughter of the Innocents*, a composition rich in movement and personalities, with a lively expressivenes, by Matteo di Giovanni, to whom we owe also the *Madonna and Saints* (1491) in the lunette; the *Madonna of the People*, amongst the most pleasing works of Lippo

25 - Palazzo pubblico.

26 - *Palazzo Sansedoni.*

27 - *Market Place*   28 - *Basilica of St. Mary of Servants.*

27

Memmi, hangs at the altar; on the right wall, *Slaughter of the Innocents*, a fresco unfortunately somewhat perished, by Pietro Lorenzetti who imagined the scene — of gloomy grandeur — in the heart of a medieval city, amongst fierce soldiers, terrified mothers and infants already dead. Some critics attribute to the same Pietro, also the damaged frescoes in the second chapel to the left of the presbytery, *Herod's Banquet* and the *Death of Saint John the Evangelist*.

Digression

He who has time can go from S. Maria dei Servi, via Val di Montone (and the oratory of the SS. Trinità, rebuilt in the XV1 th Century

with sumptious Renaissance decoration and valuable works of art including a very fine *Madonna and Child with Saints* by Neroccio di Bartolomeo) and Via Roma (at N° 27 the Society for the Execution of Pious Works with works by Siennese artists of the fourth, fiifth and sixth centuries). Thence to Porta Romana, 1327, the ponderous remains of the medieval wall (perhaps built by Agnolo di Ventura) with outer defence wall. The fresco on the external arch (on which Taddeo di Bartolo, il Sassetta and Sano di Pietro 1417-59, worked in succession) is practically illegible, while it is still possible to appreciate, unnder the arch, a *Glory of Angel Musicians*, the only known fresco by Sassetta that remains.

29 - *St. Joseph's Arch.*

29

End of the digression

From the Basilica of S. Maria dei Servi one returns by Via del Salicotto, then turns to the left into Via dei Malcontenti, across Piazza del Mercato and via Vicolo S. Salvatore to Via Duprè which goes left to the arch of S. Giuseppe, near the great edifice of the church of S. Agostino (see itinerary 4) which frames one of the most interesting views of the tower of the Mangia. Next to the arch is the sixteenth century church of S. Giuseppe, now an oratory of the Onda district, in whose museum some sculptures by the Siennese Giovanni Duprè (1817-82) are kept. Let us now return along Via Duprè to Piazza del Campo. From Piazza del Campo, via Vicolo di S. Pietro up to the Croce del Travaglio and the beginning of Via di Città which, continuing uphill, links Piazza del Campo with Piazza del Duomo. This is one of the most outstanding streets of Sienna due to its wealth of buildings and palaces, mostly of medieval origin. At the corner of Costarella dei Barberi rises the tower of the Sette Seghinelle with 4 rows of blind windows surmounted with ogival arches (from here, by Via Pellegrini one can go up directly to the Duomo. Worthy of note, at N° 18, is the Renaissance Palace Bindi-Sergardi which boasts a series of frescoes by Beccafumi dedicated to *Episodes of Roman History*, considered to be amongst the great Siennese artist's finest works).

Passing beyond the noise of the Bargello and the possibly fourteenth century Palazzo Patrizi (N° 75), headquarters of the Intronati Academy, we come in sight of the magnificent Palazzo CHIGI-SARACINI, with its curved façade that follows the sinuous winding of the street. The general structure is reminiscent of the Palazzo Pubblico, with a stone base and the upper part in brick and two rows of three-mullioned windows. The curt-off tower, from which, according to tradition, the announcement of the victory at Monteaperti was made, is also in stone.

Inside the palazzo which was partly rebuilt during the Renaissance period is the headquarters of CHIGIANA ACADEMY OF MUSIC, founded in 1923 by the Siennese Count Guido Saracini, world famous for the advanced study of music and for the important concerts held there. It is possible to get special permission to see the inside of the palazzo where the valuable collection of works of art includes works by Siennese artists of the period from 1200 to the last century and examples from other Italian schools and foreign artists.

There are outstanding paintings by Sassetta (with a masterpiece, the *Epiphany*), by Maestro dell'Osservanza, Sano di Pietro, Neroccio di Bartolomeo, Girolamo del Pacchia, Sodoma, Beccafumi, Botticelli, Salvator Rosa and Sebastiano Conca; Donatello (or del Vecchietta), Bernini (rough design in terracotta) and Mazzuoli.

Continuing along Via di Città, N° 126 is the PALAZZO PICCOLOMINI OR DELLE PAPESSE, almost certainly designed by Bernardo Rossellino. The building, now the offices of the Bank of Italy, was brought to completion between 1460 and 1465 and, because it had been commissioned by Caterina Piccolomini, sister of Pope Pius 11, was called « delle papesse ». After the restoration carried out in 1864, the similarity to contemporary Florentine architecture, in the light and dark accentuation of the exterior (first floor rustic ashlar, upper floors with Gothic mullioned windows) became clear. The corner building (which also faces Via del Castoro) is the Marsili palace (N° 132), greatly restored in 1864, designed shortly after 1350 by Luca di Bartolo Luponi of Ravenna, also in late Gothic style with brick facing lightened by a Line of Threemullioned windows.

And so we arrive at Piazza Postierla or dei Quattro Cantoni where five roads meet. At the corner of the piazza and Via Città stands the tower-house Forteguerri; on the opposite side a marble *She-wolf* (1487) recently restored, with a fifteenth century flag mast finely worked in wrought iron. Turning right into Via del Capitano, we find at the beginning the Chigi alla Postierla palace (XVI cent.), believed to have been designed by Riccio, with the interior sumptuously decorated with stucco work and frescoes, now the offices of the Superintendent of the Galleries.

Now our glance is arrested by the Palazzo del Capitano di Giustizia (presently the site of the faculty of Economic Science and Banking), restored towards the middle of 1400 and again restored to its original appearance in 1854. The lower half is in stone, the upper in brick made more graceful by Siennese arches at the bottom and double mullioned windows above, finished with a crenelated cornice. At the end of the road the magnificent Piazza del Duomo opens before our gaze.

30 - Palazzo Chigi Saracini.

Itinerary III

Piazza del Duomo - Duomo - Museum of the metropolitan works -
Baptistery - S. Maria della Scala hospital.

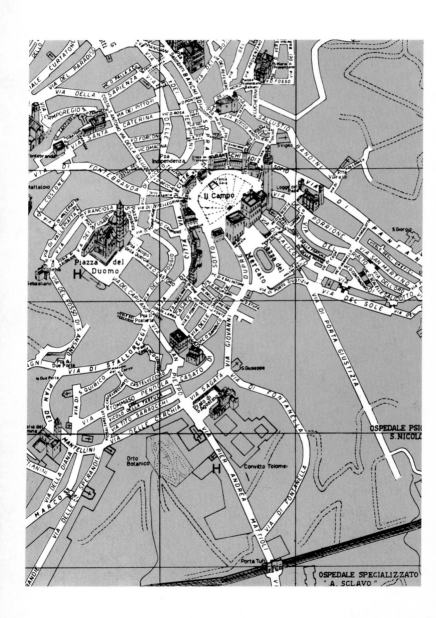

PIAZZA DEL DUOMO

Overlooking the piazza are the medieval hospital of Santa Maria della Scala, the neo-gothic Archbishop's palace, the sixteenth century palace of the Prefecture, the Gothic arcades of the new cathedral and, at the top of a flight of steps, the marble architecture of the Duomo.

31 - The Dome - Bell tower and cupola.

DUOMO

If the Public Palace is the masterpiece of Siennese civil architecture, the Duomo is that of the religious. The most illustrious visitors to the city look upon the one and the other with stupified admiration: and in the case of the Duomo it is sufficient to remember here, Taine, Ruskin and Wagner amongst the many famous names.

From the eleventh century a smdll church exercising the functions of a cathedral existed here. Towards the middle of the following century, at the dawn of the municipal age, the foundations were already completed by the second decade of 1200. The Cistercian monks of S. Galgano Abbey (one of the early Italian Gothic churches of which impressive ruins, near Siena, still remain) gave great impetus to the prosecution of the work from 1238 to 1285, when the cupola (1259-64) was built, with the apse and peribolus (1267), both later demolished. It was these monks who entrusted the building of the famous pulpit to Nicola Pisano, and to his son Giovanni, the sculptured decoration of the lower part of the façade. In the second decade of 1300 — during the government by the Nine — Siena wanted to display its new prosperity with a more grandiose prosperity, with a more grandiose cathedral to the glory of the Virgin Mary received into Heaven: for this reason the apse and crossing were demolished and the church lengthened, under the direction of Camaino di Crescentino, towards the Piatta valley (1317 cr). Then even this was not enough, they wanted a church which for size and magnificence would outdo that of their eternal rival, Florence.

This plan for a "new duomo" substantially modified the plans of the preceding church: in fact the whole of the part already built was to be only the transept to which the longitudinal aisles had to be added with the façade ("the facciatone"). This immense undertaking was begun in 1339 by Lando di Pietro, who was followed by Giovanni di Agostino and Domenico di Agostino. The works went ahead with exceptional rapidity but also at enormous cost. The plague of 1348 imposed an interruption during which time serious shortcomings in the statics of the building came to light, it had been carried out too hurriedly on ground not sufficiently prepared and hardened. The economic crisis which followed the plague and the ineffectiveness of the efforts to correct the errors already made, brought about a decision to break off the ambitious proposal. In the following decades the dangerous part of the structure was pulled down while the rest

32 - The Dome - Façade.

was used as offices for the Duomo works of art (where Iacopo della Quercia sculpted the Gaia font. The only thing left to do was to complete the old duomo: the new apse was finished in 1382, then the roof of the central nave was raised and, from 1376, Giovanni di Cecco finished the upper part of the façade.

Exterior - Facade

Stylistically the facade of the duomo combines Romanesque (the lower part) and Gothic (the upper part) aspects, but the soul of the monument, so to speak, is frankly Gothic. In fact, only the central arches are still Romanesque and they are absorbed into a whole whose articulated complexity is peculiar to Gothic architecture.

The lower part is the admirable creation of Giovanni Pisano and helpers (1284-96) but was not finished until 1333. The three doorways are surmounted by round arches (the side ones very slightly pointed) which are themselves enclosed in triangular cusps. Corner pillars (on marble plinths) frame not only the lower part but the whole front. Thin columns finely decorated with vegetable motifs flank the doorways: a bass relief by Tino di Camaino recalling the *Story of Anne and Joachim* is in the architrave of the central door. The statues and busts by Giovanni Pisano and collaborators, refer to *Figures of the Old Testament*: these are copies (the originals can be seen in the Works of Art of the Duomo Museum).

The sculptural decoration follows both a decorative and a didactic principle: in fact, the lower part of the façade was dedicated to the preparation for the advent of Mary, the upper part to her presence on earth up the time of her assumption into Heaven. Unfortunately the modifications that have been made in the order of the statues makes the reading of this theme more difficult to follow. The bronze door in the centre is a modern work by Enrico Manfrini (1958) glorifying the Madonna through references to moments in her life and the lives of biblical figures, popes, saints and artists who encouraged worship of the Virgin.

The upper part of the façade, expressing the extreme development of Gothic art, is a mass of decorative motifs: late fourteenth century statues (the originals of these are also in the Duomo Arts Museum), friezes, marquetry etc., embellish the basic structure. There is the great central rose window set in an ornate square frame (adorned by busts of *Patriarchs, prophets, evangelists* and, at the top, of the

Madonna), the two side galleries, each with five windows, separated from the framed rose window by two pillars, and the three triangular cusps, the centre one much higher than the others and with an *Angel* by Tommaso Redi (1639) on the summit. The centres of these triangular cusps are decorated with mosaics carried out by the Murano School to designs by Luigi Mussini and Alessandro Franchi (late 1800) illustrating, on the left, the *Presentation of the Virgin at the Temple,* in the centre, the *Coronation of Mary,* and on the right, the *Nativity of Jesus.*

The Siennese designer of the upper part of the façade, Giovanni di Cecco (1376), was obviously inspired by the almost contemporary façade of the Orvieto Duomo, the masterpiece of another Siennese, Lorenzo Maitani. It was the realisation of this design that was responsible for the asymmetry of the pillars flanking the frame of the rose window in relation to the two pillars at either side of the central doorway: an asymmetry which does not, however, detract from the aesthetics validity of the architectural whole.

Bell tower on the right

One follows the right wall (the left, with a single closed window is joined to the Archbishop's palace), divided by pillars crowned with pairs of fourteenth century statues (the originals are in the basement of the duomo), opened with three-mullioned windows with ogive arches under pointed cusps. The facing is horizontally striped with broad bands of white marble alternating with bands of dark marble: this decoration continues along the wall of the right transept, opened by Gothic windows, on the crossing which is joined to the baptistery and the bell-tower, erected above ahe existing structure to the design of Agostino di Giovanni and Agnolo di Ventura.

We move now to the raised pavement at the front entrance of the duomo: on the floor, three restored pictures (copies of originals by Nastagio di Gaspare, 1450) portray *Consecration Ceremonies of Ecclesiastical Dignitaries.* In the two corners at the top of the steps are two columns carrying the symbolic *She-wolf feeding the Twins*, copies by Giovanni Pisano and d'Urbano da Cortona (the originals are in the Duomo Art Museum).

Interior

Of Romanesque foundations, the interior of the duomo is Basilican, with three aisles, wide transept, apse and choir, cross-vaulted roof on central arches. The eye is attracted to the numbers of massive pillars in mixed styles which separate the aisles and continue along the two arms of the transept (26 in all): in these, the two color marble stripes we have seen onthe exterior, are repeated. A dichromatic effect which, if it restrains the impression of great height, gives a warmth and pictorial movement to the whole temple, while the polichrome of the walls, the blue and the painted stars of the roof and above all, stupendous floor, also contribute.

FLOOR

The boast of Siena Cathedral is the floor. It is divided into 56 panels, the oldest (from 1369 onwards) are graffiti, the more recent ones (up to 1547) carried out in marble (mixed marbles). The pavement portraying historical illustrations is a Gothic conception of a temple from beyond the alps, according to which every element must participate organically in the final object of glorifying the divine and preparing the way to Heaven.

Most of the subjects of the panels are dedicated to *Stories from the*

34 - *Foreshortening of Dome's façade.*

*35 - The Dome and archades 'of new
Dome from the sky.*

Old Testament (Stories of Moses, Jesus, Joshua, Abraham and Elias)
but mixed with these are some mythical figures (*Sibyls*, considered
however, to anticipate Christ) and allegorical figures (*Virtue*) besides, the only episode from the New Testament - the representation
of the *Slaughter of the Innocents*. For two centuries some forty
artists, mostly of Siena, dedicated themselves to this great artistic
work; some panels, damaged by wear over the years, have been
partly redone or substituted by copies; others, the oldest and most
prized have been covered and are only to be seen every year from
August 15 to September 15.

Let us mention here some of the most renowned artists of the designs for the execution of the pavement: Domenico di Niccolò, Matteo di Giovanni, Domenico di Bartolo, Benvenuto di Giovanni, Urbano da Cortona, Antonio Federighi, Neroccio di Bartolomeo, il Pinturicchio, and—greatest of them all for inventiveness and lively industry—, Beccafumi, who, between 1517 and 1547, produced the designs for 35 panels. To him we owe the best of the *Bible Stories*, amongst which the finest are *Moses striking water from the rock of Horeb* and the *Sacrifice of Abraham*, both in the presbytery, and the *Sacrifice of Ahab*, under the cupola. Particular attention is due also to the *Allegory of Fortune*, by Paul Mannucci on a Pinturicchio cartoon (central nave), the *Erythreaen Sibyl* by Antonio Federighi (right aisle), the *Emperor Sigismund on the Throne* by Domenico di Bartolo (right transept), the *Allegory of Justice* by the comacine master Marchese d'Adamo and pupils (left apse), the *Slaughter of the Innocents* by Matteo di Giovanni and *Herod dethroned* by Benvenuto di Giovanni, the last two in the left transept.

Besides the pavement, another artistic characteristic of Siena cathedral, is the series of 172 imaginary busts of *Popes* (including one of *Christ*, at the end of the apse) which act as corbels for the cornice that runs along the top of the central nave and the presbytery. Placed at intervals under these busts are another 36 imaginary ones of *Eperors*, from Constantine to Theodosius: all sculptures of the fifteenth and sisteenth centuries. Close to the entrance the two finely worked holy water stoups are by Antonio Federighi (1463).

Inside the main face

The central portal is adorned by decorated columns by Giovanni di Stefano, with pedestals embellished in bassrelief of the *Stories of Mary* by Urbano da Cortona; above the door the architrave carries other reliefs dedicated to the *Life of S. Ansano* (XV cent.). The stained glass in the rose window *(The Last Supper)* was designed by Perin del Vaga and executed by Patorino de' Pastorini (1549).

Right aisle

In a niche close to the main entrance, the statue of Pope Paul V (Camillo Borghese of Siena), by Fulvio Signorini (1605). Then follow four altars decorated with seventeenth century paintings; four side doors and that to the belltower open from farther up the aisle. Above this last door is the tomb of Bishop Tommaso Piccolomini del

Testa, by Neroccio di Bartolomeo (1484-85); and at either side of the tomb reliefs by Urbano da Cortona with *Six episodes from the life of the Madonna* (particularly noteworthy is the *Annunciation*). From here we get a stupendous view of the cupola which rises up from the centre of the crossing, supported on six columns (resting against the two in the nave are the flag poles from the Carroccio di Siena (the battle wagon that carried the standards and altar and served as a rallying point at battles at that time) used at the battle of Monteaperti, 1260).

At the angles of the hexagon of the cupola, 6 columns hold 6 gilded statues of *Saints* (the four patron saints of Siena plus S. Bernard and S. Catherine) by Ventura Turapilli and Bastiano da Francesco (XV-XVI cent.).

A row of niches curves above the columns transforming the hexagon of the cupola into the dodecagono of a tambour. This last is decorating the figures of 42 *Patriarchs and prophets* painted in chiaroscuro by various fifteenth century Sienese artists. Higher still the final canopy of the cupola is decorated with false lacunars and completed with the lantern at the summit.

Right transept

As on the other side, the right transept is divided into two aisles by pillars. To the right opens the *CHIGI CHAPEL* (OR THE CHAPEL OF THE MADONNA OF THE VOWS) constructed in 1661 to a design by the renowned master of the baroque school, Gian Lorenzo Bernini at the wish of the Siennese Pope Alessandro VII Chigi. Circular and surmounted by a gilded cupola, it is a triumph of decoration. Eight columns divide it into the same number of sectors; statues, marbles, bronzes, friezes and pictures are everywhere. The picture of the *Madonna of the Vow*, by an imitator of Guido da Siena (late 1200), stands on the altar which was also designed by Bernini. The gilded bronze *Angels* which surround the *Madonna of the Vow* are believed to be the work of Bernini while the splendid statues of *S. Girolamo* and *Magdalene* in niches near the entrance are certainly his. The other statues in niches at the sides of the altar are the work of the seventeenth century Lombardy sculptors (Ercole Ferrata and Antonio Raggi) while the four bassreliefs above (*Stories of Mary*) were executed in Rome in 1748. On the wall on the left, the *Visitation of the Madonna to Elizabeth*, a picture by Carlo Maratta (?late 1600) which also inspired the same artist's mosaic on the opposite wall recalling his *Flight into Egypt*.

Leaving the chapel of the Vow we shall see: on the right of the first altar, the statue of *Pope Alessandro III*, by Antonio Raggi, 1663; on the left, that of *Pope Alessandro VII*, by Ercole Ferrata, 1668, in front of which is the tombstone of the Siennese bishop Carlo Bartoli (died 1444), decorated with graffiti by Antonio Federighi

and Giuliano da Como, probably on a design by Pietro del Minella (late 1400). The altar in front of the tomb stone has an admirable canvas by the Calabrian Mattia Preti (1650 c), the *S. Bernardino Preaching*. In the angular chapel, known as the Chapel of the Sacrament, 5 fifteenth century bassreliefs executed by Giovanni Francesco da Imola (the *Evangelists*) and Giovanni di Turino (*S. Paul*), are built into the right wall; the altar is adorned with an *Adoration of the Shepherds* by Alessandro Casolani (1594).

Presbytery

Following a tradition dating from palaeochristian times, the presbytery is raised above the level of the nave. Placed there is the *High Altar* in marble, a wonderful creation designed by Baldassarre Peruzzi (1532) and carried out by Pellegrino di Pietro. A fine bronze cibourium by Vecchietta (1467-72) rests on the altar, having been brought here from the S. Maria della Scala hospital in 1506 to replace Ducci's *Maestà* (now in the Duomo Museum). At the sides two exquisite *Angel candelabra stands* by Giovanni di Stefano; the other lower *Angels* are masterly sculptures by Francesco di Giorgio Martini (1497-1499). Eight other stupendous *Angels*, the work of Beccafumi (1548-50),embellish the pillars. At the side of the altar is the bishop's residence designed by Riccio (but executed in 1907 by Tipo Corsini) to whom belong also the lectern behind the altar, and higher up, the chancel on the left (1550) while the chancel at the other side is the work of Antonio Barili and collaborators (1510).

The apse

Beccafumi's frescoes which so much brighten the well of the apse have had to be retouched and repainted to compensate for the progressive deterioration (*Apostles* 1544; *Glory of tre Trinity* 1812); seen below are Bartolomeo Cesi's *Assumption of Mary* (1595) beside two frescoes by Ventura Salimbeni (*Esther and Ahasuerus* on the right and the *Jews in the Desert* on the left) and to whom we also owe the *Figures of Saints* (1608-11). The stained glass window in the apse dedicated to the *Glorification of the Madonna* is amongst the oldest in Italy: designed by Duccio di Buoninsegna it was executed in 1288 by Siennese masters and finished nearly a century later by Giacomo di Castello. The finest monument in the apse is the CHOIR in wood which occupies the whole of the lower part

37 - Detail of the Dome's floor.

38 - The Dome - Nicola Pisano's (and his school's) pulpit.

of the well (the *'bema'* of the Byzantines). Comprising 51 stalls, it is in two adjoining parts: the centre, clearly of Renaissance influence, was designed by Riccio and carried out by Teseo di Bartolino and Benedetto di Giovanni with their collaborators (1567-70), the two sides—the most beautiful part—in Gothic style, were carried out by Francesco and Giacomo del Tonghio and helpers (1362-97) and later adorned with the finest marquetry on the backs, real masterpieces of Giovanni da Verona (1503) which came from the ex monastery of S. Benedetto outside the Tufi gate (Monteoliveto minore).

Sacristy

On the left of the entrance door hangs a small holy water basin in gilded bronze, white marble and enamel, a wonderful example of the jeweller's art, by Giovanni di Turino (1437).
Among the many works of art, the following are particularly noteworthy: the remains of frescoes by Domenico di Bartolo and, in the three chapels, by Nicola di Naldo (right chapel), by Gualtiero di Giovanni (central chapel) and probably by Benedetto di Bindo (the left chapel), all early 1500. From the chapel on the left one passes into the vestibule where a bust of *Alessandro VII*, by Melchiorre Caffà, valid pupil of Bernini, stands. In the next capitular room are some paintings by Sano di Pietro, note the pleasingly characteristic faces, costumes and places in the *S. Bernardino preaching in Piazza del Campo.*

Left transept

Near to the pillars of the cupola our admiring gaze falls on the thou--sand times famous *PULPIT* by Nicola Pisano and his assistants amongst whom was his son Giovanni, Arnolfo di Cambio, Donato and master Lapo (1266-68). Octagonal, in marble, it is an absolute masterpiece of Romano-Gothic sculpture, or better still, of all time. In this work, the serene and classical composure of Nicola seen in the first two panels gives way to the palpitating *pathos* of his son Giovanni for whom "the events narrated are no longer merely contemplated but become one with the spirit of he who recalls them" (Stefano Bottari). These events are: the seven *Stories of the Gospels* carved in bass-relief on the panels of the parapet of the pulpit in the following order:
1) The *Nativity and Visitation*; 2) *Arrival of the Magi and Adoration of the Magi*; 3) *Jesus Presented at the Temple, Joseph's Dream and*

39 - *The Dome - Piccolomini Library.*   40 - *Piccolomini Library -* The Three ▶
Graces.

39

Flight into Egypt; 4) *Slaughter of the Innocents*; 5) *The Crucifixion*;
6) *Final Judgement of the Reprobates*; 7) *Final Judgement of the
Chosen.* These seven *Stories* are separated by statues of *Prophets* and
Angels. The eighth side of the octagon is occupied by the stairs which
have been remade to a design by Riccio. The sides of the parapet rest
on trilobe arches (in the spandrels are more statues of Prophets)
separated in their turn, by statues of *Virtue.* Marble columns with
Corinthian capitals support the arches. The bases of thin columns
are alternately stylobate, lions tearing animals to pieces and liones-
ses tearing animals to pieces (an ancient symbol, this, of the church
triumphing over paganism). The pedestal of the central column, to

41 - Piccolomini Library - A miniated choir-book.

contrast, is carved in a group of bass-reliefs of *Allegories of the seven liberal arts and music.*

Side chapel of S. Ansano (opposite the chapel of the Sacrament). At the altar, a canvas by Francesco Vanni (*S. Ansano baptises the people of Siena* 1596), on the left wall, *MONUMENTAL TOMB OF CARDINAL RICCARDO PETRONI*, a notable work by Tino di Camaino (1317-18), the finest Siennese sculptor after Jacopo della Quercia (helped in this work by his father Camaino di Crescentino). Above the base resting on brackets, four caryatids hold the sarcophagus decorated with reliefs inspired by the Gospel. The bier, with the statue of the bishop protected by an awning held up by angels, rests on the sarcophagus. The monument—of great solemnity—is completed with a shrine with statues of the *Madonna and Child* and the *Saints Peter and Paul.* Another outstanding work of art in this chapel is the bronze dedicated to *Bishop Pecci,* by Donatello (1426) embedded in the pavement (kept covered).

Outside the chapel, placed symmetrically with respect to the statues

42 - *Piccolomini Library - Il Pinturicchio,* Enea Silvio Piccolomini Receives from Frederic III the Crown of Poet.

43 - Museo dell'Opera del Duomo (Museum of the Dome's Opera) - Giovanni Pisano's Hall.

44 - Giovanni Pisano's Hall - Iacopo della Quercia - Vergin with Child, St. Jerome and Offerer.

in the opposite arm of the transept, are the statues of *Pius II*, by Giuseppe Mazzuoli (1698) and *Pius III*, by Pietro Bolestra (1706). On the floor is a graffito funeral slab of 1468. Then follow two altars, in the second is a *Crucifixion* in wood, traditionally believed to have come from the Carroccio of Siena.

The Renaissance CHAPEL OF S. GIOVANNI BATTISTA, designed by Giovanni di Stefano (1482), is entered via a marble portal carved with prodigious finesse by Lorenzo Marrina and flanked by two orders of 2 columns superimposed one above the other (the bases, at one time believed to be Roman, are perhaps, instead, the work of Antonio Federighi). The wrought iron gate is by Sallustio di Francesco Barili. The chapel is abundantly decorated with stuccoes by Alberto Caponeri and Cosimo Lucchi (1596) and has a baptismal font with reliefs probably by Federighi. All the ornamentation of the lower part of the chapel is of particular importance. From the left: fine *Portrait of Alberto Aringhieri when young, keeper of the cathedral works of art* by Pinturicchio (1504); *S. Ansano*, statue by Giovanni di Stefano (1487); *Nativity of John the Baptist* by Pinturicchio (1504); statue of *John the Baptist*, admirable example of the later Donatello (1457), an expression of profound spiritual torment; Pinturicchio's *Beheading of S. John the Baptist*, redone by Francesco Rustici called il Rustichino (1608); *S. Catherine of Alessandria*, a delicate sculpture by Neroccio di Bartolomeo and pupils (1487); *Portrait of Alberto Aringhieri when old*, by Pinturicchio. In the upper part of the chapel is Pinturicchio's *S. John the Baptist in the Desert.*

In a niche on the right outside the chapel, is a statue of *Marcantonio Zondadari*, by Giuseppe and Bartolomeo Mazzuoli (1725).

The left aisle

One is struck immediately by the magnificent prospect of the PICCOLOMINI LIBRARY constitued by a double marble arch elegantly worked by Marrina (1497); in the right arch is a small altar with a bass-relief of *S. John the Evangelist* by Giovanni di Stefano (under the altar, a wooden *Pietà* by Alberto di Betto); in the left arch, which is the entrance to the library, is a double bronze gate by Antonio Ormanni (1497). The *Coronation of Pius III* by Pinturicchio is in the large lunette above the entrance. The Piccolomini Library was constructed at the wish of cardinal Francesco Todeschini Piccolomini, then Pope Pius III (1495), for the safe-keeping of the

precious library of his uncle Pope Pius II. Pinturicchio, fellow disciple if Raphael at the school of Perugino, was called to Siena to embellish it. According to tradition, Raphael is said to have given Pinturicchio cartoons and sketches for the various compositions.

The work, executed between 1505 and 1507 by the master already over 50 (with many helpers), confirms his particular qualities: richness and vividness of colour, a taste for decorative elegance and pleasing narrative.

In the rectangular hall paved with majolica with the arms of the Piccolomini (1507), the ten Pinturicchio frescoes, divided by strips of "grotesque" decoration (entwining figurative and geometrical motifs which continue on the spandels) represent, starting from the end window on the right: 1) *The young Enea Silvio Piccolomini leaves for the Basle Council*; 2) *As ambassador of the Council to the Court of King James of Scotland*; 3) *He receives the Poets' crown of Laurel from the emperor of the Sacred Roman Empire Federico III*; 4) *Sent as ambassador of Federico III to Pape Eugenio IV*; 5) *As Bishop of Siena, he presents Federico III to his fiancée Eleonora of Portugal at Porta Camollia*; 6) *Nominated cardinal by Pope Callisto III*; 7) *Elected Pope with the name of Pius II*; 8) *At Mantova he exhorts congress to undertake a crusade agains the Turks*; 9) *He decrees the canonization of S. Catherine of Siena*; 10) *At Ancona he exhorts congress to hurry the departure for the crusade (which never takes place)*.

The painting of the mythological and allegorical subject of the roof is the work of Pinturicchio's pupils, in the centre is the arms of the Piccolomini. In the centre of the library, above the marble pedestal attributed to Federighi, are statues of the THREE GRACES, third century Roman copy of a Greek original, magnificent for the delicate elegance of the harmoniously entwined figures. On the carved benches placed underneath the frescoes, fine miniatures in precious corals made by famous fifteenth century artists such as Liberale da Verona, Girolama da Cremona, Sano di Pietro, Guidoccio Cozzarelli, Benvenuto di Giovanni, are displayed. Above the entrance to the library, the *Adam and Eve Expelled from Paradise*, excellent copy of one of the reliefs on the Gaia font (which see); between the windows is a statue in bronze of *Christa resurrected*, by Fulvio Signorini (1595). Leaving the library we move along the left aisle, here we see a Bandino Bandini monument surmounted by a sculptured group (*Jesus resurrected and two angels*) the work of a master of the

45 - *Museo dell'Opera del Duomo - Duccio di Boninsegna, Crucifixion (panel of* Majesty).

46 - *Museo dell'Opera del Duomo - Duccio di Boninsegna*, Majesty *(front-part)*.

Michaelangelo school (1570c) and, farther on, the PICCOLOMINI ALTAR, an extremely mature work of Andrea Bregno (1503), remarkable for its exquisite elegance: the statues in the niches (the *Saints Gregory, Paul, Peter and Pius*) are early works of Michaelangelo (1501-4) who also possibly finished the *S. Francesco* begun by Torrigiani; the statue in the upper niche (the *Madonna*) has recently been attributed to the young Jacopo della Quercia; the marble framed picture (*Madonna of the Milk*), a work of tender sentiment is perhaps by Paolo di Giovanni Fei (1381). Next come three altars with paintings by Pietro Sorri (late 1500) and Francesco Trevisani (late 1600) and, against the internal face, the statue of *Pope Marcello II*, by Domenico Cofaggi.

Leaving the duomo we pass along the left side, in sight of the

superb structure of the "new duomo" (1339-1355). This comprises part of the principal façade "il facciatone", the right aisle (which is attached to the duomo) with five enormous arcades of all shapes (and opened in the outward facing wall by a single window); a part of the left side with three arcades and blind windows with single openings set in the wall of the palace of the Prefecture. From what we can see it is possible to imagine the incomparable grandeur of the work if it had been finished, and its great artistic quality: one can see, for example, the decoration by Giovanni d'Agostino, also the designer of the very beautiful side door (1345).

In the first three closed arcades of the right aisle the Metropolitan Museum of Art is located.

METROPOLITAN MUSEUM OF ART

Since 1870, many of the most precious works from the cathedral have been arranged and preserved against decay and dispersion in this museum (with many additions and continual modifications in the criteria). The visit is therefore of the greatest interest.

Ground floor

Is constituted by a single large hall divided in two by fifteenth century iron gates from the S. Maria della Scala hospital.

In the first area, examples of sculpture from various sources: high-reliefs of the late 1200; front of a Roman sarcophagus; marble pluteus carved by a pupil of Giovanni Pisano (possibly Lapo); spires from the cathedral; plastic works by Urbano da Cortona; a lion by Giovanni Pisano.

Some marble spires by Nicola Pisano's pupils are placed against the gates dividing the room. Immediately behind, two she-welves which were originally on the columns opposite the façade of the cathedral: the one on the right claimed to be by Giovanni Pisano, that on the left by Urbano da Cortona. A masterpiece by Jacopo della Quercia stands out in the middle of this second area, the high-relief portraying the *Madonna and Child, S. Girolamo and the cardinal Antonio Casini as a donor kneeling in Prayer*, amongst the latest of Jacopo's sculptures, previously located in the duomo of Siena. In the floor, funeral slabs by Tommaso Pecci (XIV cent.) and broken fragments of the original floor of the duomo (notably the *Age of man* by Federighi, 1475, and the *Paleotestamentary episodes* by Beccafumi).

Of extraordinary artistic value are the TEN STATUES BY GIOVANNI PISANO placed against the pillars, originally on the façade of the duomo (1284-96). Outside any stylistic influence, in these the artist has expressed his genius, rich in human and mystical impulses, with figures "all sudden, intense and passionnate movement" (Stefano Bottari). From the left the statues represent: *Moses, Moses' Mary* (the most famous), *Simeon*, a *Sibyl, Isaiah, Balaam, David, Habakkuk, Plato, Solomon*. Other statues by pupils of Giovanni Pisano are amongst the various pillars; on the wall on the left, pieces of sculpture from the rose window of the duomo: the *Madonna and Child and Christ's forebears*, perhaps the work of Giovanni di Cecco (1377c); at the bottom, two *Bulls* and a *Horse* by Giovanni Pisano; on the end wall, *Baptism of Christ*, an altar piece by Andrea and Raffaello Piccinelli called the Brescianini (1524) influenced by Andrea del Sarto, and placed on a Baroque altar.

First floor

The whole left wall of the Duccio room is devoted to the MAESTÀ by Duccio di Buoninsegna, the first masterpiece, in order of time, of the glorious Siennese paintings of the fourth century. It was carried out in only three years between 1308 and 1311 and when the work which is painted on both faces was completed, it was greeted enthusiastically by numbers of the people and political and religious authorities. Placed on the main altar of the duomo, it remained there until 1505 when, at the wish of Pandolfo Petrucci, it was removed (to be replaced later by Vecchietta's ciborium). In 1771 it was decided to separate the two faces and put them on two altars in the duomo. The great altar-piece suffered serious damage which was only partly repaired and, later, lost to foreign collections 8 partitions of the predella, besides the loss of some lesser elements and the crowning (perhaps composed of two panels). Originally the altar-piece had 60 panels dedicated to the *Glorification of Mary and events taken from her life and the life of Jesus.* This work represents the greatest achievement of Duccio's final maturity. Much has been written about his various stylistic leanings (late Byzantinism, contemporary Siennese art, Cimabue, Giovanni Pisano, Giotto and, according to some people, French miniatures) but, let us conclude with Pier Paolo Donati who writes: "the altar-piece remains the swan song of an ancient figurative civilization" (the Byzantine) "reduced during the centuries to the purely mechanical and revived, for the last time, at the hands of a true artist who performs the miracle of sublimating the cultural facts to pure poetry".

On the end wall of the room is the front of the altar-piece with the paintings, *Madonna and Child enthroned between ten Angels and Saints Peter, John the Baptist, Agnes, Paul, John the Evangelist, Agatha and the four protectors of Siena.* The busts of *Ten Apostles* are painted along the top of the picture. A Latin inscription on the step of the Madonna's throne says: "O Saintly Mother of God, grant peace to Siena and life to Duccio who has painted thee thus". In this face of the altar-piece the Byzantine influence is made sharply evident by the search for a means to enliven the static figures, and by the tenuous germinating of harmonious colours as a *pianissimo* in Gregorian chant.

The entrance wall: the back of the altar-piece: *26 Episodes of the Passion.* At the bottom: *The Entrance into Jerusalem; The Washing of the Feet; The Last Supper; Christ's Farewell after the Supper; The Kiss of Judas; The Prayer in the Garden of Olives; The Capture of Christ; Peter Denies Christ; Christ before Anna; Christ before Caiphas; The Flagellation; Christ before the Magistrates; Interrogated by Pilate.* At the top: *Christ replies to Herod; Christ again before*

47 - The Baptistry

48 - Scala Sabatelli (Sabatelli's staircase).

Pilate; The Flagellation; Christ Crowned with Thorns; Pilate washes his Hands; The Way to Calvary; The Crucifixion; Deposition from the Cross; TheEntombment; The Holy Women at the Tomb; The Descent into Hell; Magdalene appears to Christ; The Meeting at Emmaus.

Left wall: fragments of the predella and of the crowning (19 small panels with Stories of Christ and of the Virgin and 4 Prophets). All these Stories on the back of the altar piece reaffirm the inventiveness which characterises Duccio's work: every scene is a sublime work culminating with the Crucifixion.

Right wall: a triptych of Pietro Lorenzetti's latest period (The Birth of the Virgin 1324) of the highest quality (often imitated), and the Madonna and Child, an early work by Duccio.

We proceed, through a door on the right, to a room adorned with cabinets designed by Riccio (XVI cent.), then to another room with a collection of 8 ancient manuscripts in miniature, from the fourth and fifth centuries (from the Duomo and the S. Maria della Scala hospital) a testimony to the artists who made contributions to the fabric of the Duomo with projects, designs etc.

Returning to the hall of the Maestà through a door on the left, we enter a room (note the double window of the new duomo) where cartoons of Siennese artists of the last century, concerning the pavement of the Duomo, are displayed with sketches for the mosaics on the façade, and, under glass, coral miniatures of 1300 and 1400.

We enter a room on the left where the TREASURE is kept, this is a collection of sacred objects and works of art of immense value. The reliquary of the Head of Saint Galgano in gold embossed silver with filigree and enamels (late 1200) is particularly admirable also a wooden Crucifixion by Giovanni Pisano surrounded by pictures of the Madonna and S. John the Evangelist by Giovanni di Paolo; the painted wood busts of the Saints Crescenzio, Victor and Savino, by Francesco di Valdambrino (1409).

Second floor

Hall of the "Madonna with the large eyes" - The picture in the centre, painted and partly in relief, gives its name to the room. It is a Madonna and Child of the first half of the third century, to which the Siennese prayed before confronting the battle of Monteaperti. On the left wall: Four Saints, part of a polyptych by Ambrogio Lorenzetti; 9 pictures of the Articles of the Creed attributed to Nicola di

49 - The Baptistry - Baptismal Font.

50 - The Baptistry - Baptismal Font,
Lorenzo Ghiberti - Jesus' Baptism.

Naldo; a ciborium, painted and gilded during 1500; Giovanni di Paolo's *S. Girolamo*; 4 coffin covers by Sodoma. The following works are the most artistically valuable in the room (deposited here temporarily by the church of S. Agostino): the triptych of the *Blessed Agostino Novello and Four of his Miracles*, an example of the last works of Simoné Martini (1330c) possibly helped by Lippo Memmi. In this work Simone's typical "linear" lines are clearly defined by an analytical separation between the various figurative elements, the sharp outlines of the design and the plastic association of architecture and landscape.

To continue the tour of the wall: Cupboard doors painted by Benedetto di Bindo and his pupils (1411-12); *Madonna and Child*, perhaps by Sassetta; *Apparition of S. Francis at the Capitol of Arles*, by Giovanni di Paolo; paintings by Gregorio di Cecco, Matteo di Giovanni, Sano di Pietro, and of a pupil of Duccio called Maestro di Città di Castello.

On the left from the landing, one enters the "saloncino dei conversari" (the little conversation salon) (where Alfieri read some of his tragedies in 1777), this too is decorated with works of art by Siennese and Tuscan masters of the XV-XVII centuries, amongst which a vigorous *S. Paul* by Beccafumi (1515-16) stands out.

In the next room, wall hangings in cloth, sacred vestments and a variety of works of art are displayed.

Leaving the museum one passes under the high portal that opens at the end of the "new duomo", descends the steps known as "Sabatelli's" (because they are the work of Giovanni Sabatelli, 1451), and arrives in Piazza Saint Giovanni.

BAPTISTERY

The piazza is dominated by the high front of the baptistery, sheer below the apse of the duomo. The edifice was constructed in 1312-25 but the façade was only completed in 1382 perhaps to a design by Giacomo di Mino del Pelicciaio. Besides the baptistery it covered part of the apse of the duomo and the upper part remained incomplete (it has been restored recently). The polychrome marble of the duomo façade is copied here but in a more severe style. The three large portals are surmounted by arches in full centre (the middle one a cuspidal arch). Between the portals and at the corners of the façade large elegant pillars are decorated by small arches. The lower part of the front is distinguished from the upper (where three blind acute

51 - The Baptistry - Baptismal Font,
Donatello - Herod's Banquet.

52 - The Baptistry - Baptismal Font,
Donatello - The Faith.

arch windows are set) by a series of hanging ogee arches. In the pavement outside the entrance, 3 graffiti illustrating the *Sacrament of Baptism* are breaking up: two were designed by Antonio Federighi (1451) and the one on the left by Gartolomeo di Maiano (1450).

Interior
The interior, probably to designs by Camaino di Crescentino and Tino di Camaino was completed around 1325. It is a rectangular hall divided into 3 aisles by 2 rows of pillars, covered with a cross-vault roof and finished with a polygonal apse. Roof, apse and two lunettes above the side altars are covered by frescoes of about the middle of 1400, mostly by Vecchietto and his school. Next to the entrance a holy water stoup carved by Federighi (1482); in a niche in the left hand wall is a wonden statue of the *Baptist* by a disciple of Jacopo della Quercia. In the middle of the baptistery, raised on two steps, one can admire one of the most beautiful works of Tuscan Gothic sculpture of the Renaissance. THE BAPTISMAL FONT almost certainly designed by Jacopo della Quercia (1416-34) and constructed by Pietro del Minella, Bastiano del Corso and Nanni di Luca (1428-30), consists of a six sided bowl on which rests a ciborium, also hexagonal, surmounted by a small column with capital and another small terminal column with the statue of the Baptist resting on its capital. By a master sculptor in Jacopo's circle. All the sculptural decoration was done by the most celebrated masters of the fifteenth century in Tuscany.
The bowl of the font. Every one of the 6 faces carries a bass-relief in gilded bronze separated by statues. Starting from the side opposite the altar and proceeding to the right: 1) *Zachariah is turned out of the Temple*, a forceful composition by Jacopo della Quercia, 1417; statue of *Justice* by Giovanni di Turino, 1224; 2) *Birth of John the Baptist* by Turino di Sano, 1427; statue of *Charity* by Giovanni di Turino, 1424; 3) *John the Baptist preaching* by the same, 1427; the statue *Prudence*, by the same; 4) *Baptism of Christ*, an elegant, harmonious creation by Lorenzo Ghiberti, 1427; stupendous statue of *Faith* by Donatello; 5) *The Capture of John the Baptist* a scene of limpid clarity by Ghiberti, 1427; mystical personification of *Hope* by Donatello (1428); 6) *Herod's Banquet*, a masterpiece by Donatello (1427) comparable for artistic excellence, with the most famous reliefs on the altar to the Saint at Padua; statue of *Fortitude*, by Goro di Neroccio, 1428.

Ciborium - In the niches: 5 figures of *Prophets* carved by Jacopo della Quercia and *Madonna and Child* by Giovanni di Turino. Above the cornice: 4 bronze *Angels* (two by Donatello and two by Giovanni di Turino, 1424).

We leave the baptistery. The palace to the right on the corner of the piazza is the palace of the Magnifico, so called because it was constructed in 1508 by Domenico di Bartolomeo of Piacenza (to a design by Cozzarelli) for Pandolfo Petrucci, magnificent lord of Siena from 1502 to 1512. Cozzarelli's bronze rings and ornaments on the façade are a copy (the originals are in the National Gallery). Of the frescoes which adorned the great staircase, some are in the National Gallery, others in foreign collections.

Back in Piazza del Duomo, a glance should be given to the buildings not yet seen. In front of the duomo is the long façade in stone and brick decorated with bifore mullioned windows, of the very ancient *S. Maria della Scala Hospital* (? IX cent.), restored around the beginning of 1300, and still preserving some features of this period. The interior, laid out as a hospital, boasts some noteworthy works of art amongst which the series of frescoes in the Pellegrinaio hall is of particular historical-documentary interest, a rare pictorial patrimony unfortunately in abandonment. Most of them were executed by Domenico di Bertolo (1440-43) and are dedicated to the glorification of the charitable works which Siena promoted in aid of orphans and the sick.

From the hospital is is possible to approach the church of S. Maria della Scala or the Annunziata, built in 1252 but rebuilt in 1466 by Guidoccio d'Andrea. It has a coloured lacunar ceiling and a number of works of art amongst which the more important are: the organ carved by Ventura di ser Gerolamo Turapilli (beginning of XVI cent. ?), possibly to a design by Baldassarre Peruzzi (at the end of the right wall: the other organ, also by Turapilli is simpler); the beautiful bronze statue of *Christ Risen*, by Vecchietta, 1476 (high altar); the *Probatica piscina* (1732) painted by Sebastiano Conca in the well of the apse; the choir carved in wood by Ventura Turapilli (1490). Next to the church, under the hospital vaults is the oratory of the Company of S. Catherine of the Night, it was arranged in this way in 1700 and still preserves the cell in which S. Catherine rested after comforting the patients in the nearby hospital. A terracotta by Vecchietta (1461) of *S. Catherine Sleeping* is kept in the cell. There are other works of artistic interest in the sacristy.

Adjoining the last is the oratory of the Confraternity of the Flagellants, with examples of the work of Sienese masterartists of the XIV-XVI centuries amongst which is a *Sacred Family* by Sodoma (1520). Back in Piazza Duomo, again towards the right, is the palace of the Prefecture, built in 1498 and greatly enlarged by the Medici towards the end of 1500, to a design by Buontalenti (it was the governor's office), then on several occasions later it received further embellishment; and, on the left, the Archbishop's palace, amongst the finest

53 - *The Baptistry - Federighi's holy water stoup.*

54 - *The Baptistry* - St. John the Baptist (*Iacopo della Quercia's school*).

53

54

examples of neogothic architecture in Italy (1718-23). The interior, decorously ornate, decorated with a masterpiece of Ambrogio Lorenzetti: the *Madonna of the Milk*, a very human version of an old Byzantine pictorial theme, returned to fashion during 1300.

Taking Via dei Fusari and Vicolo S. Girolamo on the left of the Archbishop's palace, we go down to a widerning of the road overlooked by the imposing side of the hospital. Here is the little Renaissance church of S. Sebastiano in Valle Piatta, now the oratory of the contrada (district) of Selva, decorated inside with the paintings of sixteenth and seventeenth century masters and a fifteenth century terracotta relief of the *Madonna*, placed above the high altar.

Itinerary IV

National Gallery - Church of S. Agostino.

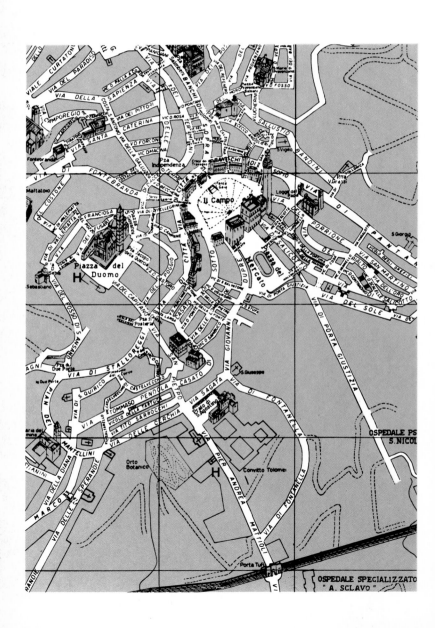

From Piazza del Campo we take Via di Città, and on reaching Piazza Postierla, turn left into Via S. Pietro where, at N° 29, we find the palazzo Buonsignori, built around 1450 according to structural and stylistic canons taken from the Palazzo Pubblico. This is amongst the most impressive and refined examples of Gothic civil architecture in Siena and the home of the National Gallery.

THE NATIONAL GALLERY

The gallery originated in the second half of the eighteenth century with Abbot Ciaccheri's collection, then was enlarged by numerous private legacies and works from religious orders suppressed during the time of the Lorraine, of Napoleon and the newly constituted realm of Italy. Today it is the greatest collection of Siennese paintings of the period from 1200 to 1600, in the world, and comprises more than 700 paintings hung in 37 rooms. In this collection we have a clear demonstration of the progress of painting from the Byzantinian beginnings to the advent, between the end of 1200 and the early 1300, of the great masters already mentioned, Duccio, Simone and the two Lorenzetti—whose influence, although with a great variety of digressions, continued until late 1400, that is to say, to the Renaissance style first and later to mannerism and baroque. To those mentioned above we must add the other outstanding names: of the late 1300, Taddeo di Bartolo; of 1400, Sassetta, Giovanni di Paolo, Neroccio di Bartolomeo, il Vecchietta, Francesco di Giorgio Martini; of 1500, Beccafumi and Sodoma; of 1600, Rutilio Manetti. Here we must limit ourselves to mentioning—in the endless series of works— only the most important of the names and examples.

The number preceding the work refers to the number in the catalogue. At the present time, some rooms are undergoing re-arrangement.

The elegant courtyard of the palace is adorned with sculptures and fragments of sculpture, mostly from 1300. In a room on the right, bronze rings by Cozzarelli from the Magnifico palace. Then one goes up to the second floor.

Second floor

Room 1 - 1, Panelled frontispiece (*The Redeemer and symbols of the Evangelist* at the centre, at the sides, three *Stories of Christ and three Stories of a Saint* representing the first work (dated 1215) in Siennese painting to show the Romanesque influence; 8, Frontispiece with *Three scenes from the Passion*, by Guido da Siena (c 1280), following the more mature examples of Byzantine painting, and amongst the first paintings on canvas instead of wood; *Painted Cross*, from the end of 1100 or the beginning of 1200, and so is amongst the oldest examples of Siennese painting. Also, thirteenth century paintings of the Guido da Siena school.

Room 2 - 15, *S. Peter enthroned* and 6 *Stories* (of the *Madonna and of S. Peter*), a work of high quality by Guido da Siena and pupils (influenced by Cimabue); 9-13, *Stories of Christ*, possibly the side panels of the *Maestà* by Guido da Siena in the Palazzo Pubblico; 14, *S. John the Baptist enthroned and 12 Stories of his life*, a frontispiece of the Siennese school (1270-80 c.) inspired by oriental miniatures. Other works by Guido da Siena, of his school and by Margaritone d'Arezzo.

Room 3 - 47, *Madonna and Child, Saints, Prophets and Patriarchs*, a polyptych by Duccio di Buoninsegna and pupils, a sharply clear design with intensely expressive figures; 28, *Madonna and Child with Saints*, a Duccio polyptych of strong religious feeling; *Madonna of Mercy*, by Nicolò di Segna, responsible also for the *Crucifixion*, 1345 (N° 34). Works by Ugolino di Nerio and the school of Duccio.

Room 4 - 20, *"Madonna of the Franciscans"*, one of Duccio's most famous paintings, on wood (1300 c), a work of musical rythm on a background of small geometrical patterns (Provence influence); 583, *Madonna and Child*, of the school of Duccio. Works by Ugolino di Nerio, 34, *Crucifixion with S. Francis*, Maestro di Città di Castello, Maestro di Badia a Isola, Segna di Bonaventura.

Room 5 - 104, *Adoration of the Magi* by Bartolo di Fredi (about 1320-80), more eccentric than the great XIVth century Siennese painters, in his tendency to sacrifice plasticity to a certain crudeness of design: this is his masterpiece for the festive animation of the theme and brilliance of colour. There are other worthy works by Bartolo here, along with a beautiful polyptych, N° 51 by Luca di Tommé and Niccolò Tegliacci (1362).

Room 6 - *Madonna and Child*, by Simone Martini, an example of the master's finest style; 595, *Madonna and Child*, an admirable painting by Lippo Memmi, brother-in-law to Simone. Other works by Niccolò di Buonaccorso, Nadda Ceccarelli and pupils of Simone Martini and Lippo Memmi.

Room 7 - 77, *Madonna and Child and Saints Mary Magdalene and Dorothy*, by Ambrogio Lorenzetti (1330 c.): the hollowcheeked S. Dorothy offers fleur-de-lis to the Madonna; 70-71, *View of a City on the Sea* (? Talamone) and *View of a Castle beside a Lake* (? Trasimeno): these are the oldest European paintings of landscapes (cupboard or chest fronts?), sharply drawn and of almost romantic nostalgic magic; 65, *Madonna and Child, Saints, Doctors of the Church and Angels*, a sublimely poetical work by Ambrogio Lorenzetti, where the painting makes music of the harmony of the colours, and in the melody of the lines (much imitated since); *Madonna and Child*, Ambrogio Lorenzetti's loving homage to maternity; 88, the

55 - Picture-gallery - Duccio di Boninsegna, Vergin of Franciscans.

Annunciation, a scene of serene charm by Ambrogio Lorenzetti (1344); various elements of the monumental altar piece painted by Pietro Lorenzetti for the church of Carmine di Siena (1329) and later broken up: Here we have the central part (*Madonna and Child between S. Nicola da Bari and the Prophet Elias*), at the sides, the *Saints* (62, 64, *Thaddaeus, Bartholomew, Thomas and James*) and the predella (*Stories of the Carmellite order*). This marks, perhaps, the height of Pietro's maturity, not only for the regal majesty of the Madonna's face, but also, and mainly, for the little *Stories* which are particularly to be admired for their gem colours, for the great attention to detail and the bold perspective and spatial imagination; 116, *Birth of the Virgin and Saints*, by Paul and Giovanni Fei (1380-90) clearly inspired by that by Pietro Lorenzetti now in the Museum of the Cathedral Works. The same room houses other works by Pietro and Ambrogio Lorenbetti and their pupils (amongst whom the above mentioned Ugolina Lorenzetti), Paolo di Giovanni Fei, Maestro di S. Pietro Ovile, Giacomo di Mino del Pellicciaio and a statue of the Baptist by Domenico di Niccolò dei Cori.

Room 8 - Works attributed to Pietro Lorenzetti (an outstanding *Madonna and Child with 4 Saints* Nº 50), by masters influenced by Duccio di Buoninsegna and Simone Martini, by Andrea Vanni (note Nº 114, *Crucifixion and Prophets*) and by Maestro of the Maestà in London.

Room 9 - 164, *Madonna and Child and Angel Musicians*, by Domenico di Bartolo, 1433, one of the artist's finest works (he decorated the hall of the Pellegrinaio at the S. Maria della Scala hospital, with frescoes) stylistically—as Enzo Carli says—already showing signs of Renaissance painting; 171, *Mystical marriage of S. Catherine of Alessandria, S. John the Baptist and S. Anthony the abbot*, a delicious example of the work of Michelino da Besozzo (Varese), exponent of the so-called "international gothic" much diffused in Europe in the first decades of the fifteenth century, influenced in this work by Stefano da Verona. Other works by Niccolò di Pietro Gerini, Bernardo Daddi, Lorenzo Monaco (157 *Madonna and Child with Saints*), Rossello di Jacopo Franchi, Spinello Aretino, Giovanni del Bindo and, perhaps, by Antonio Veneziano.

Room 10 - Works by Paolo and Giovanni Fei. In the adjoining chapel, a damaged polychrome statue (the *Magdalene*) attributed to Cozzarelli.

Room 11 - Works by Taddeo di Bartolo, a pupil of Bartolo di Fredi

56 - Picture-gallery - Ambrogio Lorenzetti - Vergin with Child, Angels and Saints.

56

57 - Picture-gallery - Ambrogio Lorenzetti (?) - View of a Town on the Sea.

but often closer to the style of Lorenzetti, he lived between the end of 1300 and early 1400. Noteworthy are: the paintings N°s 127, 128, 132, 133, the *Crucifixion* (N° 55) and the *Annunciation* (N° 131) clearly inspired by Simone Martini. Other works by Martino di Bartolomeo and Andrea di Bartolo.

Room 12 - Works by Giovanni di Paolo, a complex, pictorial per-

sonality, with a vocation, one minute almost miniaturistic, and another magnificently synthetic, sometimes grave and solemn, sometimes simple and affectionate, but always with a relish for the "tense and cutting" line (Carli) typically his own. Of special note: 200, *Crucifixion*, 1440, where souls and gestures seem petrified by suffering; 212, *Christ suffering* and *Christ triumphant*, early works; 189,

57

Assumption and Saints, the last work dated (1475); 174, 175, 176, *Presentation of Mary at the Temple, Crucifixion, Flight into Egypt*: the last picture demonstrates the free, lyrical fantasy of style in this master's landscapes.

Room 13 - Works by Giovanni di Paolo and Stefano di Giovanni, called the Sassetta, the greatest fifteenth century Siennese artist who seems to have combined the ideas of the XIV th century with the formal application already typical of the Renaissance. Particularly: by Giovanni di Paolo, 172, *Last Judgement, Paradise and Hell*: a scene narrated like a fable, with malicious little episodes in *Hell* and affectionate courtesies in the *Paradise*; 206, *Madonna of Meekness* (1445 c), the Virgin is seated in an apple orchard with a background of a small circle of idealized peaks similar to the cusps on a crown; 211, the *Presentation of Jesus at the Temple* with an architectural arrangement similar to the *Presentation* N° 654. Il Sassetta is represented by parts of a grandiose polyptych painted for the chapel of the wollen arts arts (1423-26), later broken up and partly dispersed: 167, *The Last Supper* (note the perspective), 166, *S. Anthony the abbot beaten by devils* (with a stupendous landscape), and figures of *Prophets, Doctors of the Church and the 4 Patron Saints of Siena.* Also by Sassetta is a Madonna and Child with two Angels (N° 325) unfortunately damaged. There are also: 177, *Madonna and Child with Saints*, a small triptych by Maestro dell'Osservanza, of a delicacy that recalls Sassetta; 203, *S. Bernardino*, by Pietro di Giovanni di Ambrogio, considered to be a life-like portrait of the Saint distinguished by the vigorous drawing of every line and wrinkle of the face.

Room 14 - By Neroccio di Bartolomeo: 281, *Madonna and Child and Saints Girolamo and Bernardino* (c 1476) the most spiritual, almost ethereal of his *Madonnas* present in this room (very lovely also are: 282, *Madonna and Child between S. Michael and S. Bernardino*, 1476, and 295, *Madonna and Child, Magdalen and the Baptist*). By Matteo di Giovanni: 286, *Madonna and Child and Angels*: a smile barely touches the face of the Mother as she contemplates the chubby Child being honoured by the Angels; 280, *Madonna and Child and Saints John the Evangelist and James* another delicate painting by the same master. By Francesco di Giorgio Martini: 277, *Annunciation*, a pictorial masterpiece by this versatile Siennese genius who was also an excellent military architect and valid sculptor; 437, *Nativity with Saints Bernardino and Thomas d'Aquinus,* 1475 with the figures standing out as if sculpted; 288, *Madonna and Child and an Angel*, 1472 c, somewhat influenced by contemporary Florentine painting. Other works by Matteo di Giovanni, Francesco di Giorgio Martini and a beautiful example of the work of Guidoccio Cozzarelli (367, *Madonna and Child and Saints*, 1482).

Room 15 - Works by Neroccio di Bartolomeo, Pietro di Domenico, Andrea di Niccolò and in the corridor, by Girolamo di Benvenuto and Maestro dell'Osservanza.

Rooms 16, 17, 18 - Given over entirely to the works (mostly large polyptychs) of Sano di Pietro, the most fertile *Siennese* painter of the fifteenth century, an excellent craftsman, with an easy narrative style although not particularly inventive. Note: N° 237, the *Madonna and Child* of the triptych (1470 c); 265, *S. Girolamo in the desert*, the *Stories of Saints Cosma and Damian*, on the predella of the triptych N° 233 (c. 1465), *The Madonna recommends Siena to Pote Callistus III (1456)* and 246, *the Madonna and Child, the Blessed Colombini and 4 Saints* (1444).

Room 19 - Francesco di Giorgio Martini, 440, *Coronation of the Virgin* (1472), a grandiose altar-piece, filled with people, all sparkling with colour. Works by Lorenzo di Pietro called the Vecchietta, a painter at first attracted to the Florentines but who later returned to the linearistic Siennese tradition, but interpreted with restraint: we see also the doors for a cupboard for relics ("arliquiera") of 1455 (N° 204) and the painting N° 210, amongst his latest creations (towards 1480). Works by Giacomo Pacchiarotti, Bernardino Fungai, Benvenuto de Giovanni (N° 434, *Ascension of Christ*).

Third floor

In the great hall, pictures previously in other rooms of the gallery are displayed with those from the Spannocchi collection, which was donated to the gallery. Besides numerous important paintings of *Flowers*, *Still life*, *Portraits*, by Dutch and German masters, some particularly pleasing ones are: *S. Girolamo*, by Albrecht Duerer (1514) *Portrait of Charles V*, by Christopf Amberger and *Herodius receives John the Baptist's Head*, by a pupil of Altdorfer. For number and quality of the works, the Lombardo-Venetian schools are amongst the first in Italy: the most striking: Lotto's *Birth of Jesus*, two portraits by Moroni, the grandiose *Rape of Europa* by Padovanino. There

58-59 - *Picture-gallery* - *Up: Giovanni di Paolo,* Flight into Egypt *(a detail). Down: Bartolo di Fredi,* Magi's Homage.

are also some very fine works by artists of other schools, such as Girolamo Mazzolo Bevoli, Cavalier d'Arpino and Bernardo Strozzi.

First floor

Room 20 - 309, *Annunciation* by Girolamo da Cremona, a skillful miniaturist (his corals can be seen in the duomo) admired also by the local artists (as Matteo di Giovanni). Works by Benvenuto di Giovanni and Pacchiarotti.

Room 21 - Closed at the present time.

Room 22 - Works by Bicci di Lorenzo, Matteo Balducci and the Florentine Cosimo Rosselli.

Room 23 - 493, the *Sacred Family and S. Giovannino*, by Pinturicchio, where a certain conventionality of line and figures is redeemed by the delightful landscape. Works by Matteo Balducci, Bernardino Fungai, Girolamo Genga, Girolamo di Benvenuto and Giacomo Pacchiarotti.

Room 24 - Works by Ventura Salimbene, Rutilio Manetti, Giuseppe Bazzani and Antiveduto Grammatica (the Mora players).

Room 25 - Houses a masterpiece by Rutilio Manetti, the most important Siennese painter of the seventeenth century who, after trying various other influences, moved into the orbit of Caravaggio, but with his own feeling for light, colour and form: *S. Eligio and the plague-stricken*, 1631 (N° 626).

Room 26 - 61, *The Vestal, Tuccia defends her innocence*, a grandiose composition by Manetti.

Room 27 - Works by Innocenzo da Imola, Mariotto Albertinelli of Florence, Giorgio Vasari and other Tuscan masters.

Room 28 - 650, 651, 652, *Charity, Hope and Fortitude*, three pictures of great inventive freshness by Andrea del Brescianino.

Room 29 - Works by Riccio and by Girolamo del Pacchia (see 410, *Annunciation* and *Visitation*, 1518), and by pupils of Beccafumi.

Room 30 - Is dedicated, on the whole, to Sodoma and Beccafumi, the most gifted Siennese painters of the first half of the XVIth century.

The first (Sodoma is the nickname of Giovanni Antonio Bazzi), after an artistic education in Milan where he assimilated teaching of the Leonardo school, stayed in Siena in Tuscany for a long time and had a large following of imitators. On the other hand, Beccafumi, nickname (derived from his patron) of Domenico di Giacomo di

Pace, called the Mecarino, was born on the outskirts of, and lived all his life in, Siena. Like Rosso Fiorentino and Pontormo, with whom he felt a certain kinship, he was a mannerist. He was distinguished, above all, by a highly personal sensitivity to the variations of light, the chief characteristic of his best works, sometimes tenuous and iridescent, sometimes so bright as to dazzle all it falls upon. Particularly outstanding in this room are: Sodoma's *Birth of Jesus* (N° 512) of about 1503, a work of the artist's youth and still in the Lombard tradition rather than of the Leonardo school, and the *Trinity and 4 Saints*, by Beccafumi, 1513 (N° 384).

Room 31 - Nearly all Sodoma's works. The best of these is his *Christ at the Pillar* (N° 352, celebrated fragment of a vast fresco (1520 c.), a fine example of the artist's full maturity, admirable for the fluency of design and flowing light and shade.

Room 32 - Still by Sodoma: 413, *Deposition from the Cross*—note the vivid expressiveness and plasticity—, and the lids of the coffins.

Room 33 - Houses famous examples of Beccafumi's work: 420, *S. Catherine receives the Stigmata*, about 1515, the artist's first large painting, influenced by the early XVIth century Florentines but already showing signs of his personal feelings on lighting; the predella of the same picture with *Three Stories of S. Catherine* (417-19) is also very lovely. Furthermore: 405, *Birth of the Madonna*, 1543, where the master gives life, in an exacting composition, to his "own restless sensations and torments" (M. Grazia Ciardi-Duprè). Works by Francesco Vanni (a fine self-portrait N° 61), Andrea del Brescianino and Sodoma.

Rooms 34-36 - are undergoing rearrangement. At present, they have Beccafumi cartoons for the pavement of the duomo, and will probably have some of the same works as before, including the beautiful *Portrait of Elizabeth of England*, traditionally attributed to Federico Zuzzari.

Room 37 - Other magnificent works by Sodoma and Beccafumi: 401, the *Prayer in the Orchard* and 433, *Christ's descent* into Hell (1525 c., both by Sodoma). Note, in the *Descent*, the figure of Eve, repeated by Beccafumi in his picture of the same subject, 1530-35 N° 427, with completely new lighting effects, however. Also by Beccafumi: 423, the *Archangel Michael and the fall of the rebellious Angels*, probably one of his last works, but in a bad state of preservation. Leaving the art gallery, a little way along Via S. Pietro is

60 - *Picture-gallery - Michelino da Besozzo*, Mystic Marriage of St. Catherine.

61 - Picture-gallery - Giovanni di Paolo, Vergin of Humility.

62 - *Picture-gallery* - *Neroccio di Bartolomeo,* Vergin with Child, St. Jerome and St. Bernardino.

63 - Picture-gallery - Francesco di Giorgio Martini, Annunciation.

64 - Picture-gallery - Il Sodoma, Jesus Christ at the Column.

N° 31, the restored Gothic "Casa della Pia" (house of the holy woman), so called because Dante's Pia of the Tolomei lived there before her imprisonment in the marsh. In the little piazza at the top of the steps, the little church of S. Pietro alle Scale, XVIIIth century restoration of a medieval building (inside, above the high altar is a stupendous *Flight into Egypt*, by Manetti, 1621, lit like a work by Caravaggio; on the left wall of the nave are fragments of a polyptych by Ambrogio Lorenzetti).

Back in Piazza Postierla, we take Via di Stalloreggi which is lined with ancient houses. On the house at the corner of Via di Stalloreggi and Via di Castelvecchio is a shrine frescoed by Sodoma (*Pietà*) called the "Madonna del Corvo" because a corvo (a raven) falling dead at this place, was seen as a fatal herald of the plague of 1348. Number 89-9L, is the house of Duccio di Buoninsegna where he painted the famous *Maestà*. Passing the arch with the two portals built into the medieval wall and decorated with a shrine frescoed by Peruzzi, one turns left into Via Piano dei Mantellini. Number 37 is the PALAZZO POLLINI-CELSI, now NERI, a simple, harmonious construction by Baldassarre Peruzzi, with ashlar plinth and brickwork above, opened by a timbered main door, balcony and double windows above, finished with an elegant cornice.

The CHURCH OF S. NICCOLÒ DEL CARMINE, all in brick, begun in 1300, was largely rebuilt by Peruzzi in 1517, and flanked by a grandiose bell tower. This stands in front of the Palazzo Pollini-Celsi. In the interior, still medieval in appearance, are the remains of frescoes (including a *Virgin Mary* attributed to Ambrogio Lorenzetti) by Siennese artists of various eras. There is an outstanding *S. Michael* on the right altar, an impressive glimpse of figures by Beccafumi, and the altar in the Chapel of the Sacrament, worked with virtuoso refinement by Marrina.

From the church of S. Niccolò del Carmine, we turn right into Via S. Marco, at the beginning of which is a house with a Romanesque door from a no longer existing church. Farther along is the church of Saints Peter and Paul, now the oratory of the contrada (district) of Chiocciola, designed by Flaminio del Turco (XVII cent.) with works by Astolfo Petrazzi and Brescianino.

We return to Via Piano dei Mantellini. At the end is the church of Saints Niccolò and Lucia, dating from the end of 1500. In the interior the roof offers a notable example of Baroque decoration by Francesco Vanni, Ventura Salimbene and other XVII century Sienese masters. There are also some paintings by Vanni Manetti, and sculptures by Cozzarelli.

An ancient gateway to the city, the Arch of S. Lucia, is in front of the church.

We return to Via Piano dei Mantellini and go straight up to the right in Via S. Quirco where, in a widening of the road we are faced with the brick front of the prison chapel of S. Ansano, joined to a stone and brick tower where, according to tradition, S. Ansano was imprisoned. Next we go along Via Tommaso Pendola to the little church of S. Antonio, of the Tartuca contrada, turning right at the end into Via S. Pietro. From there to the S. Agostino arch, once the medieval urban gateway and then out to the Prato of S. Agostino with all its trees, where the church of the same name stands.

S. AGOSTINO CHURCH

The church of S. Agostino (S. Augustine) was begun on 1258, somewhat modified at the end of 1400, and the interior transformed according to neo-classic criteria, by Luigi Vanvitelli (1755). The façade is partly hidden by an arcade that joins it to the ex-convent of S. Agostino, today home of the Tolomei institute.

Interior

Light and harmonious, with a single nave and presbytery flanked by chapels (T plan).

Of the many works of art we mention the more important. First altar on the right: *Crucifixion and Saints*, by Perugino (1506) with a limpid, smiling landscape. PICCOLOMĪNI CHAPEL - End wall: *Maestà*, by Ambrogio Lorenzetti, a recently restored fresco, the colours still vivid in those parts untouched by time. Right wall: *Slaughter of the Innocents,* by Matteo di Giovanni (1482) which recalls the picture of the same title in the Basilica of S. Maria dei Servi (the face that can be seen under Herod's arm could be a self-portrait of Matteo); at the altar, Sodoma's Epiphany (1518) all variations of light and shade with a landscape background worthy of Leonardo. Simone Martini's altar piece is now in the Duomo Museum of art. Second chapel on the right of the presbytery: the majolica pavement comes from 1488. The monochrome frescoes on the walls were uncovered recently and attributed to Francesco Giorgio Martini.

65 - *Picture-gallery - Federico Zuccari,*
Queen Elisabeth of England.

First chapel on the right of the presbytery: *Madonna and Child*, a wooden statue of the Siennese school of 1400.

High altar: an imposing marble structure in Baroque style designed by Flaminio del Turco, with statues of *Angels* by Bartolomeo Mazzuoli added in 1700. Second chapel to the left of the presbytery: *Temptations of S. Anthony*, attributed to Rutilio Manetti. Second altar on the left: Carlo Maratta's *Immaculate Conception* (1671). Third altar on the left: *Baptism of Constantine*, by Francesco Vanni. The geomineralogical and zoological museum of the Academy of Physiocrats is located in the ex-monastery of the church of S. Mustiola alla Rosa, opposite the S. Agostino church.

The Palio

It has been mentioned previously that the Piazza del Campo is noted not only for its scenic beauty but also because the famous Palio horserace is run there every year on July 2nd and August 16th.

The Palio is the only survival of all the various competitions which excited the Sienese townsfolk to passionate and often violent and bloody rivalry. Similar "games" took place in many other Italian towns, and their exacerbation by interfaction turbulence was certainly not limited to Siena. But the Palio is different from all others, which may even appear similar, in fact it is based on real local sentiments which spring from centuries old traditional loyalties to the "contrade" (districts), and sublimate them into a spectacular show. These local sentiments are an innate heartfelt "neighbourhood spirit" which is expressed not only against all other neighbourhoods but also in a positive, socially valid, internal solidarity.

The old-time Siennese "games" which have been mentioned above included: the "Pugna"—a sort of boxing all-against-all in the streets (which had to be abolished in 1325 because of the massacres it provoked); the "Mazzascudo"—jousting with mace and shield; the "Giorgiani"—fights with blunted weapons; the "Cesterelli"—a general melée wearing wicker helmets; the "Pallonata"—a contest in which the winner was the team which succeeded in throwing a large ball, launched from the Mangia Tower, into the opponent's area. In addition there were tournaments for various occasions; races with different kinds of animals, and other events. Only the Palio has survived out all these warlike contests.

The name indicated the prize, a Palium (a silk banner with a representation of the Virgin Mary), which is presented to the contrada winning the horserace in the Piazza del Campo. As will already have become clear, the Contrade are the personification of the various neighbourhoods or precincts of Siena (and anciently, also of the suburbs known as "Masse") divided among the three major zones of the town: the City (the oldest central part); St. Martin's (the south-eastern districts) and Camollia (the northwestern districts). There used to be 59 Contrade, but now there only 17 of which only 10 at a time can take part in the race for the Palio. The origin of the Contrada as a civic entity is uncertain but it is generally believed that they resulted from the transformation, after the fall of Siena in 1555, of the old parochial militia companies.

Already, however, around the middle of the fifteenth century the

*66 - Blessing of the horse of **Contrada** Capitana dell'Onda.*

67 - Town trumpeters with clarinos and musicians.

districts of Siena were segregating their followers on solemn occasions by parading behind coloured wooden structures, carried by young men and mostly representing animals (the same ones that figure on the present day banners).

Later the Contrade system began to be organised in such a way that each had its own authorised badge and clearly defined territorial limits with a headquarters, owned moveable goods and property, including its own church with religious staff, a museum with mementoes and banners celebrating past victories, and lastly a stable for the horse that would carry its colours in the race. The public life of the Contrada is regulated by a clearly defined internal hierarchy, but anyone born in a Contrada is a member of that Contrada for life, even if he leaves the city. All this was codified for the first time, by a decree dated 1730, by Violante Beatrice of Bavaria who was Regent-Governor of Siena in the Larroine period.

While there is documentary evidence of races on horses and other animals from the thirteenth century onwards, the real Palio of the Contrade, more or less in the same way as nowadays, goes back to 1660, and was held on July 2nd in honour of the Madonna of Provenzan (who miraculously appeared to Provenzan Salvani, the hero of the Battle of Montaperti who was subsequently at the Battle of the Elsa Valley Hills). The second annual race, that on August 16th which is dedicated to the Madonna of the Assumption, started in 1702.

Below is a list of the 17 Contrade, divided among the three zones of the town, and their badges and livery coulours. It should be noted that both badges and flags have been modified in various ways as regards the colours of their emblems. In particular the arms and monograms (UM) of the House of Savoy were introduced under King Humbert I (1887) and still appear on the banners.

Zone of città (the city) - 6 Districts

1) Aquila (Eagle). Banner: A double-headed eagle, crowned. Colours: Yellow, edged with black and turquoise.

2) Chiocciola (Snail). Banner: A snail. Colours: Yellow and red with blue stripes.

3) Onda (Wave). Banner: A swimming dolphin, crowned. Colours: White and sky blue.

4) Pantera (Panther). Banner: A panther rampant. Colours: Red and blue with white stripes.

68 - The Palio: the horse-race after the start.

5) Selva (Forest). Banner: An oak with a rhinoceros under it. Colours: Green and orange with white stripes.
6) Tartuca (Tortoise). Banner: A tortoise. Colours: Yellow and turquoise.

Zone of St. Martin - 5 Districts
1) Civetta (Owl). Banner: An owl. Colours: Red and black with white stripes.
2) Leocorno (Unicorn). Banner: A lion with a unicorn's horn.

Colours: White and orange with blue stripes.

3) Nicchio (Scallopshell). Banner: A scallop shell crowned. Colours: Turquoise with yellow and red stripes.

4) Torre (Tower). Banner: An elephant bearing a tower. Colours: Purple edged with white and turquoise.

5) Valdimontone (Valley of the Mountain Sheep). Banner: A ram rampant. Colours: Yellow and red with white stripes.

Zone of Camollia - 6 Districts

1) Bruco (Caterpillar). Banner: A caterpillar crowned. Colours: Yellow and green edged with blue.

2) Drago (Dragon). Banner: A dragon. Colours: Red and green with yellow stripes.

3) Giraffa (Giraffe). Banner: A giraffe led by a blackamoor. Colours: Red and white.

4) Istrice (Porcupine). Banner: A porcupine. Colours: White with red, black and blue stripes.

5) Lupa (She-wolf). Banner: A Siennese she-wolf suckling the twins. Colours: Black and white edged with orange.

6) Oca (Goose). Banner: A goose, crowned. Colours: White and green with red edging.

The costumes worn by the people taking part in the Palio recall those in fashion in Siena around the middle of the fifteenth century, and are coloured in the contrada's banner colours (except that Valdimonte contrada's costumes are pink edged with white, red and yellow). Each contrada is represented by a "team" of 9 members of the pageant: the Captain, the Drummer, two Standard Wavers, two Men-at-Arms, an Esquire, and two Flag Pages. On the occasion of the Palio the contrada's hopes are defended by a Jockey (fantino) and a Racehorse (barbero) tended by a Groom (the barbaresco) and accompanied by a Parade Horse (soprallasso) with its own Groom. Although the actual race lasts only a few minutes it is preceded and followed by a complicated cerimonial which divides the pageant into four "acts".

Preparations for the race

The preparations for the race last days (29th June till the morning of July 2nd for the first race, and 13th August till the morning of August 16th for the second). Even before these periods the Piazza del Campo is laid out for the event—the central brick paved area

69 - Contrada del Drago's page.

70 - Contrada del Lio-corno's page.

71 - Contrada della Tor-re's page.

(the "Shell") is surrounded by a protective barrier; the external part of the Piazza is filled up with wooden grandstands for the spectators (the Judges Committee has a special stand next to the racehorses' enclosure). The race track, the ring shaped area left free between the central barrier and the grandstahds, is covered with dry sand while mattresses are put on the downward facing St. Martin corner so as to lessen the effects of the frequent falls which happen to the jockeys.

The first operation is the "tratta" ("deal") or in other words the choice of the ten horses which will take part in the race and their allocation by lot to the contradas, one after the other. Six rehearsals are run during the three days prior to the race and even on the morning of the same day, to accustom the horses to the track and stimulate them to give their utmost. Should one of the horses die during this period its contrada can no longer enter for the race, but it will take its place in the historic parade, bearing the horse's hooves on a silver dish and with its banners in mourning.

During this same period the Captain of each contrada, assisted by two lieutenants who have already been busy trying to sign up the best and boldest jockeys by offering handsome retribution, enters into secret negotiations with other contrade trying to persuade them to agree to some common tactics and influence them in any way that will assure his contrada's ultimate victory.

The whole town is dressed with the flags of the districts and zones on the day of the race. At seven o'clock in the morning Mass is celebrated in the chapel in the Piazza, the standards of the contradas are exhibited in the church of St Mary of Provenzano (for the July Palio) or in the Cathedral (for the August Palio). In the afternoon each contrada's horse is blessed in the contrada's parish church. In the meantime the crowds which have gathered in the square—without counting those on balconies and roofs, at windows or any other vantage point—are concentrated into the stands or the central "shell" so as to clear the track. Recent estimates talk of 70,000 people (only some of whom have to pay) being crowded into the Piazza, while another 30,000 occupy the adjoining streets. This means that on the day of the race, Siena more than doubles its population.

The historical procession

The race takes place between 5 p.m. and 7 p.m. in the evening. Two hours seems a long time for such a short race, but most of

72 - *Contrada della Selva's page.*

73 - *Contrada dell'Onda's page.*

74 - *Contrada della Tartuca's page.*

this period is occupied in that magnificent pageant show called the Historical Procession. The procession enters the Piazza from Via del Casato and takes place according to a rigid protocol laid down following the customs of the Siennese Republic during the fifteenth century. The Procession is headed by the 6 Macebearers of the City and the City Standard Bearer (called after the Balzana) on horseback attended by a groom. 24 trumpeters and other musicians follow- the 12 silver trumpets ("called chiarine") are of a type used in the seventeenth century, and the music played is the "Palio March" composed in 1875 by Pietro Formichi. Next come 24 flag bearers from the city and the surrounding townships and castles which made up the old Siena State, followed by the banners of the major craft guilds and 102 representatives of the ancient corporations. The Captain of the People, heralded by a Squire bearing his sword and shield, comes next, on horseback and attended by a groom. The centre of the procession is formed by the "teams" of the representatives of the 10 contradas entering for the race, each followed by its Jockey on his parade horse and by its race horse led by its "barbaresco" (groom).

It is the evolutions of the "Flag Jugglers" of the Districts that give this part of the procession its animated kaleidoscopic effect. The flags are unfolded and waved back and forth and round and round in various ways and frequently tossed into the air where they turn about, thanks to the lead weight in the handle, to fall and be caught again in a continuous display of skill, imagination and fitness. After these teams come 12 City pages with laurel festoons, followed by the "teams" of the 7 contrade not entering the day's race, the Captain of Justice riding a horse led by a groom, the Captain of the Knights, 2 drummers, and a group of Knights. Last comes the Triumphal Car inspired by the City State's ancient "Battle Waggon" which followed the army into battle and whose loss was considered a dreadful omen. Drawn by 4 oxen, this great Car, finely inlaid and painted with the badges of the 17 contrade, carries the City Flag, the Banner which is the prize of the race, the bell called the "Martinella" (which was used for giving orders to the soldiers during battle), 6 trumpeters from the City Hall, and the 4 Chamberlains of the Biccherna with their attendants. The Car is escorted by 6 horsemen from the 6 districts excluded from the day's race, and by 6 horsemen of the districts (Cock, Lion, Bear, Oak, Strongsword, Viper)

75 - *The Palio - The start.*

76 - *Contrada della Pantera's page.*

which were suppressed after a riot they caused at the July Palio in 1675.

The procession completes one round of the track and takes up positions on a wooden stand facing the City Hall. The organisers of the parade arrange purposely for a studied slowness which allows for a progressive build-up of atmosphere. Every townsman passionately supports his contrada and his excitement is further fanned by the continual booming of the Sunto bell in the Mangia Tower, by loud music, by explosive sounds, the fluttering of the flags and the shouts of encouragement or sarcastic insults greeting the various "teams" as they appear.

77 - Contrada dell'Istrice's page.

The race

The "moment of truth" has almost arrived - the race itself is due. After the procession, the banner which will be the prize of the winning district is delivered to the Judge by pages, while Jockeys, the Grooms, and both horses of each district go into the courtyard of the City Hall. When they reappear, mounted on the race horses, the Jockeys are issued with whips (Nerbo) made of toughened bulls' sinews, which are used not only to encourage their own hourse but to upset rival horses or even to beat or unsaddle other jockeys - everything is allowed. The Jockeys take their places between two ropes, lining up behind the starting rope in order according to the draw.

The start (mossa) is on the dropping of the rope by the starter (mossiere). The course is three times round the track, with the winning post in front of the Judge's Box. The few minutes of the actual race are a succession of shocks, worries, excitements and disappointments, culminating in the triumph of the citizens of the winning contrada. If a Jockey falls or is thrown or pushed off his horse during the race, the horse can carry on alone and can in fact win the race without its rider.

After the race
The Jockey who has won the race and received the Palio is carried shoulder high by the men of his district, and, later on, the winners and their supporters and friends take part in a Te Deum of thanksgiving in the Provenzano Church (July Palio) or the Duomo (August Palio). At night the winning district is brilliantly illuminated and echoes with shouts of triumph and drum-rolls accompanying the contrada's banners.
On the day following the race the whole winning "team", with its race horse decorated with gilded hoofs and a sumptous train perhaps even including American style "majorettes" and with drums beating, parades the streets of Siena collecting laurels. Even then it is not finished. After the August race and after weeks of exaggerated retelling of the victory, the members of the winning contrada hold an interminable open air feast, obviously in their own district in which fortune's favourite, the winning horse, richly caparisoned for the occasion, is the guest of honour with special fodder and best sugar. And yet again there are drums, shouts, songs, illuminations and already forecasts about the next race.
Let us close this long and complex ceremony with a fine Latin motto, inspired by Verdi even if its language is weak - "Pallium, crux vel deliciae Senensium" (The Palio, cross or delight of Siena?).

© 1979 COMPAGNIA **FOTOCELERE** s.r.l./Milan
Editions R.I.S. by Italo Romboni/Siena
Photography: C. Fotocelere and Marzari/Schio
Italian text: Sandro Chierichetti
Translations: Studio Sandonà/Milan
Making-up: Renzo Matino/Schio